INTRODUCING
ISSUES WITH
OPPOSING
VIEWPOINTS®

Birth Control

Lauri S. Friedman, *Book Editor*

GREENHAVEN PRESS
A part of Gale, Cengage Learning

GALE
CENGAGE Learning™

Detroit • New York • San Francisco • New Haven, Conn • Waterville, Maine • London

Christine Nasso, *Publisher*
Elizabeth Des Chenes, *Managing Editor*

For more information, contact:
Greenhaven Press
27500 Drake Rd.
Farmington Hills, MI 48331-3535
Or you can visit our Internet site at gale.cengage.com

For product information and technology assistance, contact us at

Gale Customer Support, 1-800-877-4253
For permission to use material from this text or product, submit all requests online at www.cengage.com/permissions

Further permissions questions can be emailed to permissionrequest@cengage.com

Articles in Greenhaven Press anthologies are often edited for length to meet page requirements. In addition, original titles of these works are changed to clearly present the main thesis and to explicitly indicate the author's opinion. Every effort is made to ensure that Greenhaven Press accurately reflects the original intent of the authors. Every effort has been made to trace the owners of copyrighted material.

Cover image: © 2009 Jupiterimages.

LIBRARY OF CONGRESS CATALOGING-IN-PUBLICATION DATA

Birth control / Lauri S. Friedman, book editor.
   p. cm. -- (Introducing issues with opposing viewpoints)
  Includes bibliographical references and index.
  ISBN 978-0-7377-4334-0 (hardcover)
  1. Birth control--United States. 2. Birth control--Study and teaching--United States. 3. Sex instruction for teenagers--United States. 4. Contraceptives--United States.
  I. Friedman, Lauri S.
  HQ766.8.B57 2009
  363.9'60973--dc22
                                     2009001691

Printed in the United States of America
1 2 3 4 5 6 7 13 12 11 10 09

Contents

Chapter 3: What Restrictions Should Be Placed on Birth Control?

Foreword

Indulging in a wide spectrum of ideas, beliefs, and perspectives is a critical cornerstone of democracy. After all, it is often debates over differences of opinion, such as whether to legalize abortion, how to treat prisoners, or when to enact the death penalty, that shape our society and drive it forward. Such diversity of thought is frequently regarded as the hallmark of a healthy and civilized culture. As the Reverend Clifford Schutjer of the First Congregational Church in Mansfield, Ohio, declared in a 2001 sermon, "Surrounding oneself with only like-minded people, restricting what we listen to or read only to what we find agreeable is irresponsible. Refusing to entertain doubts once we make up our minds is a subtle but deadly form of arrogance." With this advice in mind, Introducing Issues with Opposing Viewpoints books aim to open readers' minds to the critically divergent views that comprise our world's most important debates.

Introducing Issues with Opposing Viewpoints simplifies for students the enormous and often overwhelming mass of material now available via print and electronic media. Collected in every volume is an array of opinions that captures the essence of a particular controversy or topic. Introducing Issues with Opposing Viewpoints books embody the spirit of nineteenth-century journalist Charles A. Dana's axiom: "Fight for your opinions, but do not believe that they contain the whole truth, or the only truth." Absorbing such contrasting opinions teaches students to analyze the strength of an argument and compare it to its opposition. From this process readers can inform and strengthen their own opinions, or be exposed to new information that will change their minds. Introducing Issues with Opposing Viewpoints is a mosaic of different voices. The authors are statesmen, pundits, academics, journalists, corporations, and ordinary people who have felt compelled to share their experiences and ideas in a public forum. Their words have been collected from newspapers, journals, books, speeches, interviews, and the Internet, the fastest growing body of opinionated material in the world.

Introducing Issues with Opposing Viewpoints shares many of the well-known features of its critically acclaimed parent series, Opposing Viewpoints. The articles are presented in a pro/con format, allowing readers to absorb divergent perspectives side by side. Active reading questions preface each viewpoint, requiring the student to approach the material thoughtfully and carefully. Useful charts, graphs, and cartoons supplement each article. A thorough introduction provides readers with crucial background on an issue. An annotated bibliography points the reader toward articles, books, and Web sites that contain additional information on the topic. An appendix of organizations to contact contains a wide variety of charities, nonprofit organizations, political groups, and private enterprises that each hold a position on the issue at hand. Finally, a comprehensive index allows readers to locate content quickly and efficiently.

Introducing Issues with Opposing Viewpoints is also significantly different from Opposing Viewpoints. As the series title implies, its presentation will help introduce students to the concept of opposing viewpoints and learn to use this material to aid in critical writing and debate. The series' four-color, accessible format makes the books attractive and inviting to readers of all levels. In addition, each viewpoint has been carefully edited to maximize a reader's understanding of the content. Short but thorough viewpoints capture the essence of an argument. A substantial, thought-provoking essay question placed at the end of each viewpoint asks the student to further investigate the issues raised in the viewpoint, compare and contrast two authors' arguments, or consider how one might go about forming an opinion on the topic at hand. Each viewpoint contains sidebars that include at-a-glance information and handy statistics. A Facts About section located in the back of the book further supplies students with relevant facts and figures.

Following in the tradition of the Opposing Viewpoints series, Greenhaven Press continues to provide readers with invaluable exposure to the controversial issues that shape our world. As John Stuart Mill once wrote: "The only way in which a human being can make some approach to knowing the whole of a subject is by hearing what can be said about it by persons of every variety of opinion and studying all modes in which it can be looked at by every character of mind. No wise man ever acquired his wisdom in any mode but this." It is to this principle that Introducing Issues with Opposing Viewpoints books are dedicated.

Introduction

Birth control has a long, contentious history in the United States. Whether it be diaphragms, condoms, or the birth control pill, these small devices have been considered as obscene as pornography, as dangerous as illegal drugs, and as much of a symbol of freedom and liberty as the American flag. The story of birth control in the United States is a rich, fascinating one that has played out in the nation's courts, churches, and bedrooms.

In the nineteenth and early twentieth centuries, contraception in the United States was not only prohibited, but primitive compared with the high-tech, highly effective birth control pills and latex and plastic condoms of today. Condoms then were made from animal products such as sheepskin or intestines, materials that were more porous and thus less effective at preventing pregnancy. Other common methods—such as douches, diaphragms, or the rhythm method—were similarly unreliable compared with modern birth control.

In addition to being scarce and ineffectual, birth control was socially frowned upon. The prevailing religious opinions of the day held contraceptives to be a disruption of the natural order, an interruption of what was supposed to result from married life: children. Even the nonreligious viewed contraception as dangerous in the sense that it threatened to lower the country's population—who would work the nation's factories and fight in its wars if there was a shortage of people? Even the birth control method of withdrawal was discouraged by doctors, who told their patients it caused nervousness and impotence and might even damage a woman's uterus.

Furthermore, contraception was discouraged because in those days, like some modern social movements, sex itself was discouraged. It was believed that if women did not want to bear children, they should simply refrain from having sex. Indeed, many of the early suffragists—the women who pushed for women's rights, including the right to vote—advocated abstinence and celibacy as the only appropriate form of birth control.

The nation's opinion of contraception was enshrined in the Comstock Act, which was passed in 1873. This act, variations of which were passed in twenty-four states, labeled "birth control" as an obscene item and made it a crime to distribute it or information about it. One of the strictest laws was passed in Connecticut, where the law read: "Any person who will use any drug, medicinal article or instrument for the purpose of preventing conception shall be fined not less than $50 or imprisoned not less than 60 days nor more than one year, or be both fined and imprisoned."[1]

It was in this atmosphere that a woman named Margaret Sanger fought to improve American women's access to birth control. Sanger believed that being able to control one's fertility was critical to a woman's right to achieve freedom, happiness, and independence. In Sanger's opinion, as long as women were overly burdened by child-bearing, they would have no opportunity to pursue their own education, career, or make other choices that men could more readily make. Furthermore, she saw access to birth control as a class issue—wealthy Americans tended to get around the nation's laws by importing their birth control from Europe, while poor American women had no such choice, which Sanger thought was unfair.

In 1912 Sanger began educating women about birth control by writing articles and pamphlets about contraceptives in newspapers and journals. She opened the nation's first birth control clinic in Brooklyn, New York, in 1916. There she dispensed contraceptives and information on how to use them. Sanger's activities quickly attracted the attention of authorities, however, and she was arrested multiple times for violating the Comstock Act. She spent thirty days in jail for opening the clinic. In the decades following the clinic opening, Sanger formed a variety of birth control federations, including the National Committee on Federal Legislation for Birth Control and the American Birth Control League, which later became Planned Parenthood.

Despite Sanger's advocacy, birth control remained obscene and illegal for decades. Sanger inched closer to her goal of making birth control a legal option for all American women by pushing the limits of its legality, forcing the American courts to keep reconsidering the issue. In 1932, for example, she arranged for a shipment of diaphragms to be sent from Japan to a doctor in New York. The package was confiscated by U.S. customs, however, as sending birth control through the mail was still considered illegal and obscene under the Comstock Act. Sanger helped file a lawsuit over the matter, and in

1936, in the case *United States v. One Package of Japanese Pessaries* (a term for something placed in a woman's vagina), it was determined that the federal government had no right to interfere with doctors who provided contraception to their patients. The case was a victory for Sanger, and it put American women one step closer to being able to control their fertility.

The final push for legalized birth control came in 1965, when the Supreme Court in *Griswold v. Connecticut* struck down the Comstock laws that remained on the books in Connecticut and Massachusetts. In this landmark case, the Court found that married couples have the right to use birth control as a matter of privacy. By the time of *Griswold v. Connecticut,* Sanger was eighty-six years old, and she died just a few months after the verdict, no doubt pleased that her life's goal had come to fruition. Her work for birth control rights pushed on even after her death, as *Griswold v. Connecticut* laid the groundwork for other important Supreme Court cases on reproductive rights, such as the 1972 case of *Eisenstadt v. Baird,* in which the right to use birth control was extended to unmarried people as well.

The controversy over birth control has, in recent decades, shifted from whether it should be used at all to who should be allowed to use it, focusing particularly on young people. For example, opponents and supporters of birth control frequently debate whether sex education programs should discuss it, whether teenagers should have access to it, and the extent to which parents should be involved in their teen's decision to use birth control. These are just some of the issues discussed in *Introducing Issues with Opposing Viewpoints: Birth Control.* Readers will also consider arguments about whether emergency contraception should be available, whether pharmacists have a right to decide to dispense birth control or not, and whether insurance companies should cover it. The wealth of information and perspectives provided in the article pairs will help students come to their own conclusions about the role birth control should play in American lives and what the future holds for this powerful and personal subject.

Notes
1. Quoted in *Time,* "Test for an Ancient Law," December 18, 1964. www.time.com/time/magazine/article/0,9171,876481,00.html.

Chapter 1

What Role Should Birth Control Play in Sex Education Programs?

Whether or not to include discussion of birth control in sex education classes is a controversial issue.

Teens Should Be Taught About Birth Control in School

"Making condoms available in schools does not hasten the onset of sexual intercourse or increase its frequency."

Douglas Kirby

In the following viewpoint Douglas Kirby, writer for the National Campaign to Prevent Teen and Unplanned Pregnancy, argues that teens should learn about birth control in school. The author explains that teens are under a lot of pressure to have sex, especially from their peers. As such, they are at great risk of becoming pregnant or contracting a sexually transmitted disease (STD), the author explains. However, many teens are misinformed about sex and either do not use birth control or misuse it. In the author's opinion, therefore, the best way to teach teens about birth control is through sex education programs. School-based programs can reach the most students and are especially useful for students whose parents are uncomfortable talking to their teens about birth control. The author

Douglas Kirby, "Emerging Answers: Research Findings on Programs to Prevent Teen Pregnancy and Sexually Transmitted Disease," The National Campaign to Prevent Teen and Unplanned Pregnancy, November 2007. © 2007 by The National Campaign to Prevent Teen and Unplanned Pregnancy. Reproduced by permission.

concludes that teen pregnancies and STDs can be reduced by teaching students about birth control at school.

The National Campaign to Prevent Teen and Unplanned Pregnancy is a nonprofit organization that seeks to prevent unplanned teen pregnancy by strengthening social policies and providing sex education to teens, parents, and young adults.

AS YOU READ, CONSIDER THE FOLLOWING QUESTIONS:
1. What percent of adults support comprehensive sex education programs for students, according to the author?
2. What percent of birth control education programs does the author say decreased the teenage sex rate?
3. According to the author, what positive behaviors were encouraged by sex education programs taught in schools?

Nearly all teenagers experience pressure to have sex at some time or other and therefore nearly all teens are at risk of pregnancy and STD. What causes a teen to decide to have sex or to use or not use condoms or other forms of contraception, if they do have sex? Research has identified more than 500 risk and protective factors that influence teens' sexual behavior. Risk factors increase the likelihood of pregnancy or STD; protective factors decrease the likelihood.

Effective programs change teens' sexual behavior by acting on the risk and protective factors that influence such behavior. Positive changes in sexual behavior may, in turn, result in lower rates of teen pregnancy or STD. . . .

School-Based Sex Education Classes Are Effective

Some programs focus primarily on changing the psychosocial risk and protective factors that involve sexuality: that is, teens' knowledge, beliefs, and attitudes about sex, perceived norms, their confidence in their skills to avoid sex or to use condoms or contraception, and their intentions regarding sexual behavior and the use of contraception. To be effective, such programs must be straightforward and specific; for example, they might discuss realistic situations that could lead to unprotected sex and methods for avoiding those situations, for remaining abstinent, and for using condoms and other contraceptives. . . .

Programs based on a written curriculum and implemented among groups of teens have been widely implemented in schools and elsewhere to prevent teen pregnancy and STD/HIV for many years. In addition, the vast majority of Americans support them—more than 80 percent of U.S. adults believe that comprehensive sex education programs, which emphasize abstinence, but also encourage condom and contraceptive use, should be implemented in schools.

Overall, about two-thirds of the curriculum-based sex and STD/HIV education programs studied have had positive effects on teen sexual behavior. For example, they delayed the initiation of sex, increased condom or contraceptive use, or both. Virtually all of the programs also improved sexual protective factors. The programs had mixed, but encouraging effects on reducing teen pregnancy, childbearing, and STDs. . . .

The more effective curriculum-based sex and STD/HIV education programs reduced one or more measures of sexual risk by roughly a third or more, but they did not eliminate risk. Thus, these programs alone cannot prevent all unintended pregnancy or STD, but many of them can change teens' sexual behavior and help reduce teen pregnancy and STD. They should continue to be an important part of any comprehensive community prevention initiative. . . .

Teens Respond Positively When Taught About Birth Control

Two-thirds of the 48 comprehensive programs that supported both abstinence and the use of condoms and contraceptives for sexually active teens had positive behavioral effects. Specifically, over 40 percent of the

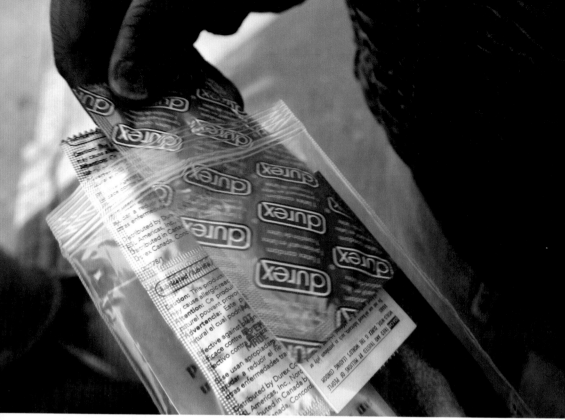

The author feels that pregnancies and STDs can be reduced by teaching teens about birth control such as condoms.

programs delayed the initiation of sex, reduced the number of sexual partners, and increased condom or contraceptive use; almost 30 percent reduced the frequency of sex (including a return to abstinence); and more than 60 percent reduced unprotected sex. Furthermore, nearly 40 percent of the programs had positive effects on more than one of these behaviors. For example, some programs both delayed the initiation of sex and increased condom or other contraceptive use.

No comprehensive program hastened the initiation of sex or increased the frequency of sex, results that many people fear. Emphasizing both abstinence and protection for those who do have sex is a realistic, effective approach that does not appear to confuse young people.

Comprehensive programs worked for both genders, for all major ethnic groups, for sexually inexperienced and experienced teens, in different settings, and in different communities. Programs may be especially likely to be effective in communities where teen pregnancy or STD and HIV are salient issues and may be less effective where these issues are not. Some programs' positive impact lasted for several years.

Virtually all of the comprehensive programs also had a positive impact on one or more factors affecting behavior. In particular, they improved factors such as knowledge about risks and consequences of pregnancy and STD; values and attitudes about having sex and using condoms or contraception; perception of peer norms about sex and contraception; confidence in the ability to say "no" to unwanted sex, to insist on using condoms or contraception, or to actually use condoms or contraception; intention to avoid sex or use contraception; and communication with parents or other adults about these topics. In part by improving these factors, the programs changed behavior in desired directions. . . .

Teens Should Have Access to Birth Control at School

Reproductive health clinics are a tried-and-true way of providing teens with reproductive health care and improving their knowledge of, access to, and skill at using condoms or other contraceptives. . . .

Clinics located in or near schools are ideally situated to provide reproductive health services to students—they are conveniently located, confidential, and free; their staff are selected and trained to work with adolescents; and they can integrate education, counseling, and medical services. Some school clinics dispense or provide prescriptions for contraceptives, and substantial proportions of sexually experienced students obtain contraceptives from them.

According to a small number of studies of mixed quality, providing contraceptives in school-based clinics does not hasten the onset of sexual intercourse or increase its frequency. But in most schools, unless clinics focus on pregnancy or STD/HIV prevention in addition to providing contraceptives, they do not increase the overall use of contraceptives markedly or decrease the overall rates of pregnancy or childbirth. When the clinics did focus on pregnancy prevention, gave a clear message about reducing sexual risk and avoiding pregnancy, and did make contraception available, they may have increased contraceptive use, but the evidence is not strong.

More than 300 schools without clinics make condoms available to students through counselors, nurses, teachers, vending machines, or baskets. In general, large proportions of sexually experienced students obtain condoms from school programs, particularly when multiple brands of condoms are freely available in convenient, private locations.

Students also obtain condoms from school clinics. According to a small number of studies of mixed quality, making condoms available in schools does not hasten the onset of sexual intercourse or increase its frequency. Its impact on actual use of condoms is less clear. . . .

Sex Education Programs Protect Teens from Pregnancy and STDs

For decades, dedicated adults have worked with teens to prevent unintended pregnancy. Their efforts have been rewarded with declining rates of pregnancy and childbirth. Prevention efforts have also resulted in lower rates of some STDs. An increasingly robust body of research is clarifying the types of behavior that most strongly affect pregnancy and STD/HIV transmission, is identifying the factors that influence sexual risk-taking and is revealing the effects of programs on teen sexual behavior and rates of pregnancy and STD. Yet pregnancy and STD rates are still high, and both more research and more effective programs are needed.

The challenge now is to continue building on these successes. Communities need to integrate what is learned from experience with what is learned from research and then use that knowledge to guide the development of more effective programs for teens. Such programs will help young people avoid pregnancy and STDs, make a more successful transition to adulthood, and prepare to be the parents of the next generation.

EVALUATING THE AUTHOR'S ARGUMENTS:

This viewpoint argues that birth control should be taught to teens in school. Consider how your school handles sex and birth control education. Are there classes on the subject? Do you think your classmates would benefit from or be threatened by sex and birth control education? Explain your reasoning and give a detailed description of the way it works in your school.

Teens Should Be Taught Abstinence and Not Comprehensive Sex Education in School

"There is ample evidence that condom-based sex education interventions do not work."

Stan Weed et al.

School is not the place to teach teens about birth control, argue Stan Weed et al. in the following viewpoint. They cite studies that show that birth control education programs do not reduce teen sex, teen pregnancy, or STD rates. In fact, Weed et al. claim that teaching students about birth control gives them the message that teen sex is acceptable, and thus actually encourages them to have sex. A more effective way to prevent teens from having sex, say Weed et al., is to teach them abstinence. In abstinence programs, students are taught that the best way to avoid becoming pregnant and infected with an STD is to choose to be abstinent—not have sex at all. Weed et al. conclude this

Stan Weed, Irene H. Ericksen, Paul J. Birch, Joseph M. White, Matthew T. Evans, and Nicole E. Anderson, "Abstinence or Comprehensive Sex Education—The Mathematica Study in Context," Institute for Research and Evaluation, June 8, 2007. Reproduced by permission.

is a much better approach to teen sexuality, and that birth control should not be taught in schools.

Stan Weed is a researcher for the Institute for Research and Evaluation. He has studied the effectiveness of abstinence education for over twenty years.

AS YOU READ, CONSIDER THE FOLLOWING QUESTIONS:
1. What percentage of all new HIV infections do the authors say is contracted by teens?
2. What were the findings of thirteen control trials of comprehensive sex education programs, according to Weed et al.?
3. What is CCU, and how does it factor into the authors' argument?

The debate about "abstinence" vs. "comprehensive" sex education has been occurring for at least three decades. The common ground that drives these competing approaches is concern about the negative consequences of adolescent sexual activity to the health and well-being of individuals and society. . . .

We have found that well-designed and well-implemented abstinence education programs can reduce teen sexual activity by as much as one half for periods of one to two years. . . .

Consequences of Teen Sex

In 2005, 63.1% of American adolescents had experienced sexual intercourse by the end of high school. Many serious health and social problems in American society are related to teen sexual activity. These include:

A. Teen Pregnancy: One in 13 high-school-age girls becomes pregnant each year in America. Adverse consequences associated with teen pregnancies include abortion, unwed teen parenthood, father absence, poverty, welfare dependence, and the growth of drug abuse, gang culture, and crime.
B. STDs: STDs have emerged as a significant threat to adolescent health. The consequences include chronic pelvic pain, genital lesions, lifetime infection, infertility, ectopic (tubal) pregnancy, damage to unborn children, cancer, and in some cases death. Adolescent STD rates are higher than rates for all other age

groups. One quarter of sexually active teens have an STD, and adolescent rates for most STDs are on the rise. The growing STD problem has been called a hidden epidemic. The direct medical cost of 9 million new cases of STDs that occurred among U.S. adolescents and young adults (15–24-year olds) in the year 2000 was estimated at $6.5 billion (in year 2000 dollars).

C. Poorer Emotional Health: There is a strong association between sexual activity and poor emotional health for adolescents.

    1. Sexually active teens are more than twice as likely as virgin teens to be depressed or attempt suicide. Adolescents report a drop in self-esteem after initiating sexual intercourse, and the majority express regret for becoming sexually active.

    2. Sexually experienced teens, especially girls, are much more likely to experience dating violence than their virgin peers, and sexual exploitation (such as statutory rape) and unwanted or forced intercourse/rape are not uncommon among sexually experienced teen girls. In 2005, one out of eight 12th grade girls in the U.S. reported being physically forced to have intercourse against her will.

Federal Funding for Abstinence Programs

Congress has spent more than 1.5 billion in state and federal dollars on abstinence-only and abstinence-only-until-marriage programs.

Funding by federal fiscal year per legislative source ($ in millions)	1982–1996	1997	1998	1999	2000	2001	2002	2003	2004	2005	2006	2007
State funding Title V, section 510 of the Social Security act			$50	$50	$50	$50	$50	$50	$50	$50	$50	$50
Community-Based Abstinence Education (CBAE)						$20	$40	$55	$75	$104	$113	$113
Adolescent Family Life Act, under Title XX of the Public Health Service Act	$4	$9	$9	$10	$10	$10	$12	$12	$12	$13	$13	$13
Other Sources									$4	$4		
Total Spent on Abstinence Education	$4	$9	$59	$60	$60	$80	$102	$117	$141	$171	$176	$176

Taken from: Marcella Howell and Marilyn Keefe, Advocates for Youth, July 2007.
www.advocatesforyouth.org/publications/factsheet/fshistoryabonly.htm.

Condoms Do Not Protect Teens from STDs

Condom use is advocated by many as the best protection for the sexually active from both pregnancy and STD transmission. Yet many consequences of teen sexual activity are not prevented by condom use.

A. Even with consistent and correct use (which is rare), condoms may diminish but do not effectively prevent STDs that are spread through skin-to-skin or skin-to-sore contact. These STDs are on the rise in the adolescent population.

B. After 20-plus years of comprehensive sex education efforts in the U.S., adolescent rates of consistent condom use are not high enough to eliminate the STDs for which condoms *are* most preventive, such as HIV, let alone STDs for which condoms are least preventive. Adolescents contract one fourth of all new HIV infections. Among sexually active U.S. teens, only 47.8% of males and 27.5% of females report using condoms consistently over a one-year period. Efforts to improve those rates have not proven successful.

C. Consistent condom use cannot prevent the negative emotional impact or the sexual exploitation and sexual violence that are associated with teen sexual activity, as described above. . . .

Teaching Students About Birth Control Does Not Work

There is ample evidence that condom-based sex education interventions do not work. In the past 20 years, studies evaluating abstinence education programs have been limited in number and in rigor, while during the same time period research on comprehensive sex education has abounded. One recent and thorough summary of this research reviewed 50 well-designed evaluation studies of comprehensive sex education programs in the United States, going back to 1990, and included these findings:

A teen celibacy group, Silver Ring Thing, sells T-shirts that promote abstinence before marriage. Many feel that abstinence education is the only way to reduce STDs and unwanted pregnancy in teens.

A. None of the programs increased the prevalence of *consistent condom use* (CCU) among adolescents for a period greater than one year. CCU is the only condom measure that approaches the stringent standard of the abstinence measure. Only one program produced a significant increase in the prevalence of CCU that was sustained for a period of one year.

B. Thirteen control trials of comprehensive sex education found no increase in teen condom use for any period of time.

C. Only two comprehensive sex education programs succeeded in improving less stringent measures of teen condom use (not CCU) for a period longer than two years, and none lasted beyond three years. . . .

Abstinence Education Is More Beneficial to Teens

Abstinence education offers benefits to adolescents and society that are not found in the comprehensive sex education approach.

A. Abstinence provides 100% protection from the biological consequences of sex (pregnancy, abortion, teen parenthood, the full spectrum of STDs).
B. Youth who abstain can avoid the negative emotional consequences related to teen sex—lowered self-esteem, regret, depression, etc.—as well as reducing the likelihood of experiencing sexual coercion and sexual violence.
C. Abstinence programs emphasize principles of self-restraint, self-esteem, future goals, long-term commitment, and unselfishness in relationships, and teach healthy relationship skills, all of which support the formation of strong marriages and healthy families.
D. Several studies have found that teaching abstinence does not reduce rates of condom use for virgin teens who become sexually active.
E. Abstinence education addresses the relationship of sexuality to the well-being of the whole person, rather than treating sexual activity as an isolated and unrelated behavior. . . .

Well-designed and well-implemented abstinence education programs can reduce teen sexual activity by as much as one half for periods of one to two years, substantially increasing the number of adolescents who avoid the full range of problems related to teen sexual activity.

EVALUATING THE AUTHOR'S ARGUMENTS:

In this viewpoint Stan Weed et al. argue that teens should not be taught about birth control in school. Instead, they suggest that teaching students about abstinence will encourage them to avoid becoming pregnant and infected with STDs. Think about your school. What method do you think would work better to protect you and your classmates from pregnancy and STDs—birth control education or abstinence education? Why? Support your answer with evidence from the viewpoints in this chapter.

Teaching Students About Birth Control Reduces Teen Pregnancy

Carmen Solomon-Fears

"An abstinence message integrated into a comprehensive sex education program ... is a more effective method to prevent teen pregnancy."

In the following viewpoint Carmen Solomon-Fears argues that teen pregnancy can be reduced by teaching birth control to students. Many teens become pregnant because they lack knowledge and understanding about sex and birth control, she says. Comprehensive sex education programs that teach these, says Solomon-Fears, should, therefore, be integrated into school curriculums. Such programs inform students about sex, including how to use birth control to prevent pregnancy. When students are taught how to use birth control, they have a better chance at preventing pregnancies. Furthermore, the author says there is no reason why students cannot learn about abstinence and birth control at the same time. In fact, encouraging them to wait to have sex and arming them with information about birth control for when they do have sex is an

Carmen Solomon-Fears, "Scientific Evaluations of Approaches to Prevent Teen Pregnancy," Congressional Research Service, May 1, 2007. Reproduced by permission.

effective strategy for reducing teen pregnancy. The author concludes that teen pregnancy rates go down when students are well informed and knowledgeable about birth control.

Carmen Solomon-Fears is a specialist in social legislation for the Domestic Social Policy Division for the U.S. Congressional Research Service.

AS YOU READ, CONSIDER THE FOLLOWING QUESTIONS:
1. About how much does Solomon-Fears say adolescent childbearing (teen pregnancy) cost U.S. taxpayers each year?
2. Name at least five characteristics of effective pregnancy prevention programs, as reported by the author.
3. What percent of adults does the author say support giving teens information about both contraception and abstinence?

Since 1991, teen pregnancy, abortion, and birth rates have all fallen considerably. In 2002 (the latest available data), the overall *pregnancy* rate for teens aged 15–19 was 75.4 per 1,000 females aged 15–19, down 35% from the 1991 level of 115.3. The 2002 teen pregnancy rate is the lowest recorded since 1973, when this series was initiated. However, it still is higher than the teen pregnancy rates of most industrialized nations.

Teen Pregnancy Has Many Long-Term Consequences

After increasing sharply during the late 1980s, the teen *birth* rate for females aged 15–19 declined every year from 1991 to 2005. The 2005 teenage birth rate of 40.4 per 1,000 women aged 15–19 is the lowest recorded birth rate for U.S. teenagers. In 2005, the number of births to teens was 421,123 (10.2% of the 4.1 million births in the U.S.), of which 6,717 births were to girls under age 15. Nearly 23% of all nonmarital births were to teens in 2005. Although birth rates for U.S. teens have dropped in recent years, they remain higher than the teenage birth rates of most industrialized nations. According to a recent report on children and youth, in 2005, 34% of ninth graders reported that they had experienced sexual intercourse. The corresponding statistics for older teens were 43% for tenth graders,

51% for eleventh graders, and 63% for twelfth graders. About 30% of female teens who have had sexual intercourse become pregnant before they reach age 20.

An October 2006 study by the National Campaign to Prevent Teen Pregnancy estimated that, in 2004, adolescent childbearing cost U.S. taxpayers about $9 billion per year. Research indicates that teens

A teenager reads a pamphlet about birth control. It is argued that teaching teens about birth control will help them make good decisions when they finally decide to have sex.

Abstinence Education Is Not Effective

A comprehensive study that followed students for more than four years found that teens who have had abstinence education are no more likely than youth who have not to abstain from sex. Furthermore, those who have had sex had similar numbers of sexual partners, were just as likely to use a condom, and initiated sex at about the same age.

Impact on Sexual Abstinence

Teens who have had abstinence education
Teens who have not had abstinence education

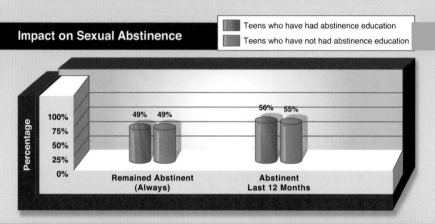

Impacts on Unprotected Sex, Last 12 Months

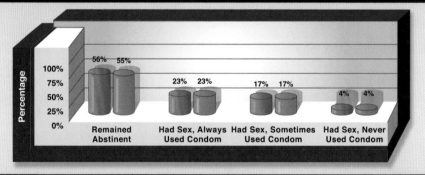

Impacts on Reported Number of Sexual Partners

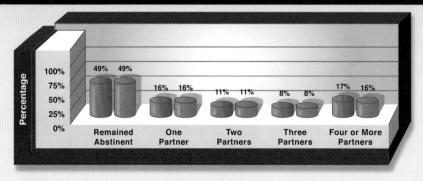

Taken from: Wave 4 Survey of Teen Activities and Attitudes, Mathematica Policy Research, Inc., 2005.

who give birth are less likely to complete high school and go on to college, thereby reducing their potential for economic self-sufficiency. The research also indicates that the children of teens are more likely than children of older parents to experience problems in school and drop out of high school, and as adults are more likely to repeat the cycle of teenage pregnancy and poverty. The 2006 report contends that if the teen birth rate had not declined between 1991 and 2004, the annual costs associated with teen childbearing would have been almost $16 billion (instead of $9 billion). In recognition of the negative, long-term consequences associated with teenage pregnancy and births, the prevention of teen pregnancy is a major national goal. . . .

Comprehensive Sex Education Helps Prevent Teen Pregnancy

Advocates of a more comprehensive approach to sex education argue that today's youth need information and decision-making skills to make realistic, practical choices about whether to engage in sexual activities. They contend that such an approach allows young people to make informed decisions regarding abstinence, gives them the information they need to resist peer pressure and to set relationship limits, and also provides them with information on prevention of STDs and the use of contraceptives.

> **FAST FACT**
>
> A sexually active teenager who does not use birth control has a 90 percent chance of getting pregnant within one year of having intercourse, according to the California Health Council.

Based on a recent report by the National Campaign to Prevent Teen Pregnancy, there are five random assignment experimentally designed studies (published since 2000) of teen pregnancy prevention programs that have been proven to be effective in delaying sexual activity, improving contraceptive use among sexually active teenagers, and/or preventing teen pregnancy.

Many analysts and researchers agree that effective pregnancy prevention programs have many of the following characteristics:

- Convince teens that not having sex or that using contraception consistently and carefully is the right thing to do.

- Last a sufficient length of time.
- Are operated by leaders who believe in their programs and who are adequately trained.
- Actively engage participants and personalize the program information.
- Address peer pressure.
- Teach communication skills.
- Reflect the age, sexual experience, and culture of young persons in the programs. . . .

Teen Pregnancy Is Reduced When Students Are Taught Birth Control

There is a significant difference between abstinence as a *message* and abstinence-only *interventions*. While the Bush Administration continues to support an abstinence-only program intervention (with some modifications), others argue that an abstinence message integrated into a comprehensive sex education program that includes information on the use of contraceptives and that enhances decision-making skills is a more effective method to prevent teen pregnancy. A recent nationally representative survey found that 90% of adults and teens agree that young people should get a strong message that they should not have sex until they are at least out of high school, and that a majority of adults (73%) and teens (56%) want teens to get more information about both abstinence and contraception. The American public—both adults and teens—supports encouraging teens to delay sexual activity *and* providing young people with information about contraception.

EVALUATING THE AUTHOR'S ARGUMENTS:

In the viewpoint you just read, Carmen Solomon-Fears uses facts and statistics to make her argument that teaching students about birth control reduces teen pregnancy. She does not, however, use any quotations to support her point. If you were to rewrite this article and insert quotations, what authorities might you quote from? Where would you place these quotations to bolster the points Solomon-Fears makes?

Teaching Students About Abstinence Reduces Teen Pregnancy

Catholic Exchange

"A 66% decrease in teen pregnancy was due to teens choosing abstinence."

In the following viewpoint the Catholic Exchange argues that teaching students about abstinence reduces teen pregnancy. The author reports there are about 1 million teen pregnancies in the United States each year, 95 percent of which are unplanned. This rate is high, the author says, because many teens do not understand the consequences of sex, including the risk of becoming pregnant. Preventing teen pregnancy, therefore, is best accomplished by teaching teens to avoid sexual activity entirely. By waiting, says the author, teens not only learn self-control but are better protected from the dangers of premarital sex, which include becoming pregnant and contracting an STD. Because the only way to become pregnant is to have sex, the author concludes that abstinence-only programs are the best weapon against teen pregnancy.

Catholic Exchange is a nonprofit media organization that uses the Internet to connect Catholic laypeople with relevant Christian information.

AS YOU READ, CONSIDER THE FOLLOWING QUESTIONS:
1. Where are teens who have babies likely to end up, according to the author?
2. What does the phrase "slavery to our desires" mean in the context of the viewpoint?
3. What does "abstinence until marriage" offer freedom from, according to the author?

I t's been discovered. Nobody thought having "safe sex" was possible in every case. Each year 2.6 million teenagers become sexually active—a rate of 7000 per day. With high school, nearly half report having engaged in sexual activity and $^1/_3$ are currently active.

Teen Sex Hurts Society

As it turns out, teen sexual activity is extremely costly for teens and for society as a whole. From 1985–1990 alone, the federal government spent $120 *billion* on teenage childbearing. Teens who engage in sexual activity risk all kinds of costly and detrimental outcomes not limited to STD infections, emotional and psychological harm, lower educational attainment, and unmarried childbearing. All of these have direct impact on Medicare, Medicaid, government spending—and the budget.

It is known that STDs (*Sexually Transmitted Diseases*) infect approximately 12 million Americans per year, with 65,000 plagued with an incurable form. STDs are a direct cause of infertility in both men and women.

Nearly $^1/_2$ of all pregnancies as well as 1 million teen pregnancies (*95%*) are unintended, and there are approximately 40,000 new HIV infections per year. An estimated 1.3 million babies die every year through abortion, and 84% of all US abortions are performed on unmarried women. Teens who have babies out of wedlock are more likely to end up at the bottom of the socio-economic ladder. All of these numbers have huge economic implications for the country.

Birth Control Failure Rates

No birth control method protects against pregnancy 100% of the time. While some methods are better than others, the only surefire way not to get pregnant is not to have sex.

Contraceptive Method	Definition	"Typical Use" Failure Rate (percentage of females who experience an unintended pregnancy during the 1st year of typical use)
Birth Control Pill (Oral Contraception)	A hormone pill taken by mouth.	8%
Injection	A hormone injection given every 1–3 months.	3%
Emergency Contraception	An emergency high dose of birth control pills taken within 72 hours (three days) of sex.	11–25%
Intrauterine Device (IUD)	Plastic device placed inside the uterus that contains copper or hormones.	Less than 1%
Implant	Small rod inserted under the skin of a woman that releases a low dose of hormone.	Less than 1%
Male Condom	A thin, latex or polyurethane (plastic) tube that covers the penis.	21%
Female Condom	A polyurethane (plastic) tube or pouch that lines the inside of the vagina.	21%
Cervical Cap	A small rubber or plastic cup that fits over the cervix.	16–32%
Diaphragm	A round rubber dome inserted inside the vagina to cover the cervix.	16%
Contraceptive Sponge	A foam sponge containing spermicide placed into the vagina.	16–32%
Spermicide	A cream, foam, jelly, or insert placed into the vagina that kills sperm.	29%
Contraceptive Patch	A hormone patched placed on the female's skin weekly for 3 weeks (followed by 1 week off).	8%
Vaginal Contraceptive Ring	A hormonal ring placed into the vagina for 3 weeks (followed by 1 week off).	8%
Natural Family Planning/ Fertility Awareness Method	Avoiding sex near time of ovulation, when pregnancy is most likely to occur.	12–25%
Withdrawal	Male removes his penis from the female's vagina prior to ejaculation.	27%

Taken from: U.S. Department of Health and Human Services, 2008.

Abstinence Prevents Pregnancy 100% of the Time

But society has found something that works 100% of the time. We found something on which you can completely depend—much better than condoms which may work part of the time—and that's if you use them right.

The answer is easy, even though many don't want to hear it—*"abstinence until marriage."* It breaks the unwritten rule of sex on demand. It clearly illuminates the slavery to our desires so many of us face. And it emblazons the oft repeated saying, *"Why buy the cow, if the milk is free?"*

Self-control is like an immune system. People who abhor sexual-control think they are breaking free, but in reality are breaking down. Control yourself and you will not be repressed—you will be free.

Our children are *not* animals which are incapable of controlling themselves and "will do it anyway". Yet "comprehensive" sex-ed[1] teaches them that they're just that.

FAST FACT

An August 2004 study in the *Journal of Adolescent Health* discovered abstinence education resulted in a 53 percent decline in pregnancy rates among teens between ages fifteen and seventeen.

Abstinence-Only Programs Are Effective

But wait a minute, recently, a new study by the research firm *Mathematica* found that in the five programs that they studied, abstinence-instructed kids showed no statistical change in sexual behavior. So, it doesn't work, does it?

Actually this study looked at only five programs out of more than 900 in place. It was also determined the *Mathematica* survey targeted children 9 to 11 who were not evaluated until four years later. *Abstinence Education: Assessing the Evidence* found 16 of the 21 studies completed so far reported positive results, while 5 studies did not report any *significant* positive results.

---

1. Comprehensive sex education teaches students about birth control in addition to abstinence.

A group of girls belonging to an abstinence-only church program enjoy an event promoting the program's aims.

Zogby (5/8/07) found that 83% of parents think it is important for their child to wait until marriage to have sex. The *Journal of Adolescent and Family Health* concluded that a 66% decrease in teen pregnancy was due to teens choosing abstinence. The *CDC* (Centers for Disease Control and Prevention) showed a 53% decrease. But abstinence programs federally funded over the last 11 years still have many critics and several dozen Congressional abortion advocates have signed a letter to the *House Appropriations Committee* asking to cut all funds for abstinence education. According to the *CDC*, there has been a 13% decrease in the percentage of teens who have ever had sex between 1991 and 2005. Still, 17 states have rejected this funding. It's interesting to note that our government has spent $12 on the Comprehensive sex-ed/Planned Parenthood approach for every $1 spent on true abstinence projects. [Planned Parenthood] would love to zero-fund its competitors; after all abstinent kids don't spend any time in their clinics.

"Abstinence Until Marriage" Benefits Teens

As parents, our offspring are worth everything. We want to keep them from developing STDs, AIDS, HIV, going through abortions, having lower educational development, slavery . . . you name it. We have *"abstinence until marriage"* which guarantees freedom from the above. And we know simple abstinence education gives significantly better chances at helping our children escape those pitfalls. We have to demand abstinence education *and* we have to provide it ourselves.

EVALUATING THE AUTHOR'S ARGUMENTS:

This viewpoint was written by the Catholic Exchange, a religious organization. Does this fact affect the weight you give its argument? Does knowing the organization drives its values from religion convince you to agree with its views, or does it serve as a basis for you to disagree? Explain your reasoning.

Teaching Students to Use Birth Control Increases Teen STD Rates

"If kids are thinking that condoms will provide 100 percent protection from pregnancy and disease they are wrong."

Rocky Mountain Family Council

In the following viewpoint the Rocky Mountain Family Council claims that teen STD rates increase when students are taught about birth control. This is because there are many STDs that can be passed from person to person even when birth control is used. For example, condoms do not cover the entire genital region, and therefore do not protect teens 100 percent from contracting the human papillomavirus (HPV) or herpes, which are transmitted via skin-to-skin contact. In this way, says the author, birth control gives students a false sense of safety in sex. In truth, concludes the author, there is no such thing as protected sex. For this reason, the author concludes that students should not be taught birth control and are better

Rocky Mountain Family Council, "Safe and Sound: The Truth About Abstinence, Premarital Sex, and Sexually Transmitted Disease," RMFC.org, 2002. Reproduced by permission.

off learning that abstaining from sexual activity is the only guarantee they will not contract an STD.

Rocky Mountain Family Council is a nonprofit, nonpartisan education organization that works with families, churches, community organizations, and government leaders to strengthen families and marriages in Colorado.

AS YOU READ, CONSIDER THE FOLLOWING QUESTIONS:
1. Why are condoms not effective at preventing herpes, according to the author?
2. What protection does the author say condoms offer against chlamydia?
3. What makes teens unable to control their sexual urges, in the author's opinion?

The youth of America are being lied to. They are being told through the media and by their peers that sex before marriage is o.k. and that everyone is having sex. A recent study by the Centers for Disease Control and Prevention (CDC) tells a different story. CDC reported that more than half of all high school students have never engaged in sexual activity and another 13.6 percent who are sexually experienced are currently abstinent.

In a national survey, 93 percent of youth ages 12–17 said that they want a stronger abstinence message from our society.

The National Campaign to Prevent Teen Pregnancy surveyed a nationally representative sample of 501 teens ages 12 to 17 and found that 41 percent of them had had sexual intercourse. Among those who were sexually experienced, 63 percent reported wishing they had waited before becoming sexually active. . . .

Teens Are Misinformed About Birth Control

When kids lose their virginity before marriage, they put at risk their future ability to have children. They may also lose their enjoyment of sex with their spouse because of physical and emotional pain. Sexually transmitted diseases (STDs) can lead to infertility, cancer and lifelong regret. If kids are thinking that condoms will provide 100 percent protection from pregnancy and disease they are wrong. Not only are condoms not effective against many STDs, they never protect the heart from the emotional and spiritual pain of sex before marriage. . . .

HPV Is Common in America

- HPV is the most prevalent viral sexually transmitted disease (STD) in the U.S. Each year, approximately 5.5 million Americans acquire this infection. Eighty million Americans between the ages of 15 and 49 have been infected by HPV at some point in their lives.
- HPV is spread by skin-to-skin contact and the virus is frequently present throughout the genital region of infected people—including those areas not covered by a condom.
- HPV often resides in the pubic area and may be passed along during sexual contact even when condoms are used consistently and correctly.
- Genital warts are the most common clinical manifestation of HPV infection. Treatment of genital warts is often painful and may require surgical removal. Many patients with genital warts also experience

The author of this viewpoint argues that teaching teens about birth control gives them a false sense of safety since birth control does not always prevent STDs.

emotional suffering, knowing they have become infected with a sexually transmitted infection.
- A study in the *Journal of the National Cancer Institute* reported that HPV infection was present in 93 percent of cervical cancers.

Condoms Are Not Effective in Preventing Herpes

- Two types of herpes simplex virus have been identified, herpes simplex type 1 (HSV-1) and herpes simplex type 2 (HSV-2). HSV-1 is a common cause of oral herpes and HSV-2 is primarily transmitted through sexual contact—including skin-to-skin and skin-to-mucous membrane contact. Areas of transmission for males and females include the entire genital region, plus the pubic and perianal area, and the inner thigh. Since no currently manufactured condom covers all these areas of potential infection, condoms may not be highly effective in preventing transmission of genital herpes.
- A report from the American Social Health Association shows that 22 percent of Americans 12 years of age or older are infected with HSV-2. That means that approximately 45 million Americans are infected with HSV-2. Due to the fact that genital herpes is both incurable and lifelong, it may be passed to any sexual partner at any time.
- The most common symptom of genital herpes is pain at the site of infection. The pain often begins before any skin changes are visible and is typically described as "burning" or "itching." Blisters typically appear and after a week these clusters of blisters rupture to form "wet" ulcers. The ulcers become covered with a scab or crust. Other generalized symptoms include fever, headache and pain when urinating.

Chlamydia and Gonorrhea Can Lead to Infertility

- Although some who are infected with chlamydia show symptoms (abnormal genital discharge and/or painful urination), as many as 85 percent of infected women and 40 percent of infected men have no symptoms.
- Having no symptoms is very dangerous because, if left untreated, over time chlamydia can damage the reproductive system of those infected without any notice. Up to 40 percent of women infected

with chlamydia will develop pelvic inflammatory disease (PID). Approximately two-thirds of all PID is not treated, because patients have no symptoms and therefore do not know they are infected. Chlamydia, therefore, may infect a woman's reproductive organs and cause infertility without her knowing she has a problem until years later when she attempts to become pregnant.

- Condoms are inadequate safeguards for a woman's fertility because they provide unreliable protection from chlamydia.
- Chlamydia is the most common reportable infectious disease in the United States with more than 500,000 cases reported annually. It is 70 times more common than measles, mumps and whooping cough combined.
- An estimated 650,000 cases of gonorrhea (bacteria) infection occur in the U.S. each year.
- In women, the opening (cervix) to the womb (uterus) from the birth canal is the first place of infection. The disease can spread into the uterus and fallopian tubes, resulting in pelvic inflammatory disease (PID). PID affects more than 1 million women in this country every year and can cause infertility.

Sexually Active Teens Are at Risk of Contracting HIV

Approximately 50 percent of all new HIV infections occur among people under 25, with the majority being infected sexually. HIV has taken the lives of more than 350,000 Americans and millions worldwide.

Abstinence Education Effectively Prevents STDs

At what point in our nation's history was marriage taken out of discussions with our kids about sex? It was when parents forfeited their role as the primary educa-

FAST FACT

Sexually active teens account for 50 percent of all new cases of STDs, according to the Healthy Teen Network.

tor of their kids and began to leave sex education up to the "professionals." Today [2002], many teachers and parents see nothing wrong with sharing the biology of sex outside the context of marriage.

Most Birth Control Does Not Protect Against STDs

While abstaining from sex and using condoms protect against most sexually transmitted diseases (STDs), the majority of birth control methods do not provide adequate protection against STDs.

Method of Birth Control	Does This Method Protect Against STDs?
Consistent Abstinence	Yes
Birth Control Patch ("The Patch")	No
Birth Control Pill ("The Pill")	No
Birth Control Ring ("The Ring")	No
Female Condom	Yes
Male Condom	Yes
Birth Control Shot	No
Diaphragm	No
Emergency Contraception	No
IUD	No
Fertility Awareness	No
Spermicide	No
Withdrawal ("Pulling Out")	No
Not Using Any Birth Control	No

Taken from: Nemours Foundation, 2008.

However, when we teach sex as primarily a biological function, we reduce this blessing of God to mere mechanics and ourselves to mere animals. While there are biological functions that we all can benefit from knowing, it is no wonder our young people are thought not to be able to control their so-called primal urges when we treat them like animals.

When abstinence education is presented to teens in a way that provides the knowledge and skills needed to abstain from sex before marriage, the results are staggering. A program in Washington D.C. called *Best Friends* is a shining example of effective abstinence education. Only 22 percent of *Best Friends* girls reported having sexual intercourse compared with 76 percent of those Washington D.C. high school girls overall. The *Best Friends* girls had a 1.1 percent pregnancy rate, in contrast to the 26 percent pregnancy rate among high school girls city-wide.

According to The Medical Institute for Sexual Health, the *Best Friends* program shows "that a well-conceived, well-executed, long-term, comprehensive, character-based abstinence program can have a significant impact on teens."

Abstinence Offers Teens Protection from STDs

Delaying sex until marriage or abstinence is the only method supported by medical research that offers 100 percent protection from sexually transmitted diseases and early pregnancy. True abstinence is more than just delaying sex until marriage; it is understanding the role of pure sexual relations within the context of marriage.

In view of the sexually charged society we live in, it is vital for parents to talk to their teens about these issues in context. Talking about the issue of sex outside the context of marriage makes sex just a trivial pursuit, instead of the true spiritual, physical and emotional union of two people.

EVALUATING THE AUTHOR'S ARGUMENTS:

The author of this viewpoint, the Rocky Mountain Family Council, is a Christian organization that promotes a traditional view of marriage and family. Does knowing the background of the author influence your opinion of the argument? In what way?

Teaching Students to Use Birth Control Reduces Teen STD Rates

Sue Alford and Marilyn Keefe

"Given that so many students will not abstain from sex, programs have an obligation to help teens understand the risks and responsibilities that come with sex."

In the following viewpoint Sue Alford and Marilyn Keefe argue that STD rates can be reduced by teaching students to use birth control. Many teens are misinformed about birth control, especially condoms. The authors explain that teens either do not use condoms or use them incorrectly. As a result, teens acquire nearly one-half of all new STDs. Alford and Keefe think that sex education classes can teach teens how to use condoms properly in order to reduce their chances of contracting an STD. More important than teaching kids not to have sex, they say, is to encourage them to make responsible decisions when they do have sex. In this way, they can avoid STDs such as chlamydia, herpes, and HIV. For all of these reasons, Alford and Keefe conclude that teaching students about birth control can drastically reduce the teen STD rate.

Sue Alford has written numerous articles about reproductive health and planning options for adolescents that have been published by Advocates for Youth. Marilyn Keefe is the director of Reproductive Health Programs at the National Partnership for Women and Families, a nonprofit, nonpartisan group that advocates for women's reproductive rights.

AS YOU READ, CONSIDER THE FOLLOWING QUESTIONS:
1. What two components do the authors say make curriculum-based sex education most effective?
2. According to the author, what percentage of Americans think teens should learn the proper way to put on a condom?
3. Why are teens at a high risk of contracting an STD, as reported by Alford and Keefe?

The vast majority of Americans support abstinence from sexual activity for school-age children, especially younger adolescents. Yet, abstinence-only-until-marriage programs, currently being taught in many schools, are at odds with what most Americans want schools to teach. The public supports a broad sex education curriculum that stresses abstinence as the best way to avoid unintended pregnancy and sexually transmitted infections (STIs) [or STDs] but that also conveys complete and medically accurate information about contraception and condoms. . . .

Teens Are Misinformed About Sex and STIs

Many abstinence-only curricula contain "false, misleading or distorted information." A 2004 investigation by the minority staff of the House Government Reform Committee reviewed 13 commonly used abstinence-only curricula taught to millions of school-age youth. The study concluded that two of the curricula were accurate but that 11 others, used by 69 organizations in 25 states, blurred religion and science, and contained unproven claims and subjective conclusions or outright falsehoods regarding the effectiveness of contraceptives, gender traits, and when life begins. Among the misconceptions and outright falsehoods:

- A 43-day-old fetus is a "thinking person."
- HIV can be spread via sweat and tears.
- Half of gay male teenagers in the United States have tested positive for HIV.
- Pregnancy can result from touching another person's genitals.
- Condoms fail to prevent HIV transmission as often as 31 percent of the time in heterosexual intercourse.
- Women who have an abortion "are more prone to suicide."
- As many as 10 percent of women who have an abortion become sterile.

Government has an obligation to provide accurate information and to eschew the provision of misinformation. Such obligations extend to state-supported health education and health care services. By providing misinformation and withholding accurate information that youth need to make informed choices, abstinence-only-until-marriage programs violate youth's basic human right to sexual health information, are ethically unsupportable, and inherently coercive. Health care providers and health educators have ethical obligations to provide accurate health information. Patients and students have a right to receive the most accurate and complete information—information that will allow young people to achieve good health outcomes. Current federal abstinence laws and guidelines are ethically problematic because they limit the information—including accurate information about contraception and safer sex—available to young people. . . .

FAST FACT

The Centers for Disease Control reports that 3.2 million teen girls in the United States contracted an STD from having unprotected sex.

Comprehensive Sex Education Teaches Teens About Birth Control

Considerable scientific evidence demonstrates that programs that include information about both abstinence and contraception can work to help

Parents Want Students to Be Taught About Birth Control and STDs

A poll by the Kaiser Foundation, National Public Radio, and Harvard's Kennedy School of Government found that STDs and how birth control can protect against them were among the topics that most parents thought were appropriate to discuss in school sex education classes.

Topic	Appropriate				Not Appropriate
	Total Appropriate	Middle School	High School	Both	
STDs other than HIV/AIDS	99%	9%	15%	75%	1%
HIV/AIDS	98%	9%	11%	78%	1%
How to talk with parents about sex	97%	12%	8%	77%	2%
Basics of how babies are made	96%	14%	13%	69%	3%
Waiting to have intercourse until older	95%	10%	12%	73%	4%
How to get tested for HIV and other STDs	94%	5%	33%	56%	4%
Birth control	94%	8%	29%	57%	5%
How to deal with emotional issues and consequences of being sexually active	94%	7%	23%	64%	5%
Waiting to have sexual intercourse until married	93%	8%	13%	72%	7%
How to talk to a girlfriend/boyfriend about "how far to go" sexually	92%	6%	23%	63%	6%
How to make responsible sexual choices based on individual values	91%	9%	21%	61%	8%
How to use and where to get contraceptives	86%	5%	37%	44%	12%
Abortion	85%	5%	30%	50%	13%
How to put on a condom	83%	5%	38%	40%	15%
Masturbation	77%	8%	22%	47%	19%
Homosexuality and sexual orientation	73%	5%	24%	44%	25%
Oral sex	72%	4%	29%	39%	27%
That teens can obtain birth control pills from family planning clinics and doctors without permission from a parent	71%	3%	40%	28%	28%

Taken from: Kaiser Foundation, NPR, Kennedy School of Government, 2004.

teens delay sexual activity, have fewer sexual partners and increase contraceptive use when they begin having sex. Although there is no one silver bullet, effective programs include curriculum-based sex education that includes information about *both* abstinence and contraceptive use. Other effective approaches include youth development programs whose primary focus is to engage young people constructively in their communities and schools. Another approach, shown to be effective with girls, combines health care, academic assistance, comprehensive sex education, participation in performing arts and individuals sports, and employment assistance. . . .

The Public Supports Teaching Teens About STIs

The public prefers comprehensive sex education to abstinence-only-until-marriage programs by a wide margin. According to a poll, conducted in 2003 by the Kaiser Family Foundation, National Public Radio, and Harvard University, only 15 percent of Americans believe that schools should only teach abstinence from sexual intercourse and should not provide information on condoms and other contraception. A 2007 poll of voters conducted by the National Women's Law Center and Planned Parenthood Federation of America yielded remarkably similar results, with more than three out of four respondents preferring comprehensive sex education curricula, while only 14 percent favored an "abstinence-only" approach.

Americans expressed support for a broad sex education curriculum that teaches about abstinence as well as the "basics of how babies are made." In addition,

- 99 percent of Americans wanted programs to cover other STIs as well as HIV.
- 98 percent wanted youth to learn all about HIV and AIDS.
- 94 percent wanted youth to learn how to get tested for HIV and other STIs.
- 93 percent wanted youth to be taught about "waiting to have sexual intercourse until married."
- 83 percent wanted youth to learn how to put on a condom.
- 71 percent wanted youth to know that "that teens can obtain birth control pills from family planning clinics without permission from a parent."

The Kaiser poll also found that that a substantial plurality (46 percent) believes that the most appropriate approach is "abstinence-plus." These Americans felt that schools should emphasize abstinence but should also teach about condoms and contraception. Thirty-six percent of those polled believed that abstinence is *not* the most important thing, and that sex education should focus on teaching teens how to make responsible decisions about sex. . . .

To Reduce STIs Teens Must Be Taught About Birth Control

Given that half of teens have had sex, even when educators encourage them not to, sex education must be driven by public health principles rather than ideology. Sex education may promote abstinence as the

Because condoms are effective at preventing pregnancy and the spread of STDs, the authors feel it is important to educate teens on their use.

best option for teens. But given that so many students will not abstain from sex, programs have an obligation to help teens understand the risks and responsibilities that come with sex. Survey after survey indicates that adolescents have a tremendous unmet need for information related to sexuality, contraception, STIs, and making sexual decisions. Government-sponsored programs need to fill this information gap, not cause it to worsen.

A nationwide survey conducted by the Kaiser Family Foundation and *Seventeen Magazine* revealed considerable gaps in teens' knowledge. The survey found that many teens hold misconceptions and harbor unnecessary and unfounded fears—such as the belief that contraception can cause infertility or birth defects. Nearly 20 percent of surveyed teens underestimated the effectiveness of the contraceptive patch or ring, and over 25 percent believed that emergency contraception causes abortion. Few teens understood the effectiveness of the male condom in preventing STIs, including HIV. In addition, over 25 percent of the teens did not know that oral contraception provides no protection against sexually transmitted diseases. The government-sponsored abstinence evaluation conducted by Mathematica Policy Research also confirmed that teens have important gaps in knowledge of STIs. The study found that on average, youth got only about half the answers correct regarding the health consequences of STIs.

Public health statistics confirm the need for more, not less, information and services directed at adolescents. . . .

- Approximately a quarter of teen females and 18 percent of teen males did not use a method of contraception at first intercourse.
- The interval between the time an adolescent female starts sexual activity and seeks health care services is approximately 12 months. . . .
- Adolescents are at higher risk for acquiring STIs for a combination of behavioral, biological, and cultural reasons. The higher prevalence reflects: 1) multiple barriers to accessing quality STI prevention services, including lack of insurance or other ability to pay; 2) lack of transportation; 3) discomfort with facilities and services designed for adults; and 4) concerns about confidentiality.

- An estimated half of all new HIV infections occur in people under age 25.
- Recent estimates suggest that while representing 25 percent of the ever sexually active population, 15- to 24-year olds acquire nearly one-half of all new STIs.

EVALUATING THE AUTHORS' ARGUMENTS:

In this viewpoint Sue Alford and Marilyn Keefe argue that teaching students about birth control helps reduce STD rates among the teen population. How do you think the author of the preceding viewpoint, the Rocky Mountain Family Council, might respond to this argument? Explain your answer using evidence from the texts.

Chapter 2

Should Access to Birth Control Be Controlled?

Many feel that prescription birth control should be just as available as birth control sold over the counter.

Pharmacists Should Be Allowed to Refuse to Fill Birth Control Prescriptions

Doug Bandow

"If contraceptives are available like other medicines, no doctor should have to write a prescription nor any pharmacist have to fill one."

In the following viewpoint the author argues that pharmacists have the right to refuse to fill prescriptions based on moral beliefs. He contends that choice should be a privilege allotted to everyone, including pharmacists and medical professionals, regardless of the government's stance. Just as it is a woman's choice to choose whether she takes an emergency contraceptive or not, so too, says Bandow, should a pharmacist be able to choose not to dispense a medication that he or she disagrees with. The author concludes that laws that inhibit a pharmacist's right to execute his belief by refusing to fill a prescription are wrong.

Doug Bandow is vice president of policy for Citizen Outreach and the author of *Leviathan Unchained: Washington's*

Doug Bandow, "Freedom to Choose: What's Good for the Goose Is Good for the Gander," *Human Events,* June 2, 2005, Copyright © 2005 Human Events Inc. Reproduced by permission.

Bipartisan Big Government Consensus, and former special assistant to President Ronald Reagan.

AS YOU READ, CONSIDER THE FOLLOWING QUESTIONS:
1. What does the author believe advocates of government action fear?
2. What does the word "inimical" mean in the context of the viewpoint?
3. What does the author suggest the government do in order to increase access to contraceptives?

Abortion, gay marriage, euthanasia and the like are among today's most contentious political issues. Choosing sides often isn't easy.

For instance, no one should feel comfortable about the state rebuffing a woman's desire for an abortion. But the procedure destroys a human life.

What should be a simple decision is allowing individuals to say no, irrespective of the government's stance. If abortion is legal, no doctor should have to perform it. If assisted suicide is permissible, no medical professional should have to participate.

If gay relationships are left untouched by the authorities, no apartment owner should have to rent to a same-sex couple. If contraceptives are available like other medicines, no doctor should have to write a prescription nor any pharmacist have to fill one.

In short, if "choice" is good, it should be protected for everyone. Unfortunately, however, many liberal interest groups seem to believe that choice means allowing them to choose for everyone else.

> **FAST FACT**
>
> Four states—Arkansas, Georgia, Mississippi, and South Dakota—have "conscience clause" laws that allow pharmacists to refuse to fill prescriptions for birth control.

The latest cause celebre involves pharmacists who won't fill prescriptions for birth control or the "morning after" pill. Illinois Gov. Rod Blagojevich has required pharmacies to fulfill birth control prescriptions. Three states are considering legislation to do the same.

Advocates of government action fear citizens acting on their beliefs. Worries columnist Ellen Goodman, "how much further do we want to expand the reach of individual conscience?"

Apparently the primary social problem today is too many people caring too much about virtue.

Goodman believes one set of moral presumptions should trump those of everyone else. Someone engaging in an activity thought to be morally wrong has a right to aid and support from others.

What of someone who believes that abortion or contraception is inimical to their commitment to heal the sick? In Goodman's view, they are asking for "conscience without consequence."

They could just quit their jobs, she says. Which in the case of doctors and pharmacists presumably means leaving their professions.

What if people don't follow Goodman's advice? Coerce them. Chris Taylor of the Planned Parenthood Advocates of Wisconsin demanded "a strong penalty" for pharmacist Neil Noesen who refused to fill a birth control prescription.

Pharmacist Rich Quayle stands out front of the Walgreens in Highland, Illinois, where he refused to dispense the "morning after" pill for religious reasons.

American Opinions on Whether Pharmacists Should Be Able to Refuse to Fill Birth Control Prescriptions

While the majority of Americans believe pharmacists do not have a right to withhold birth control prescriptions, Republicans are the group most likely to support such an action.

Question: "Should pharmacists who personally oppose birth control for religious reasons be able to refuse to sell birth control to women who have a prescription for them, or shouldn't pharmacists be able to refuse to sell birth control pills?"

Affiliation	Should Be Able to Refuse	Should Not Be Able to Refuse	Unsure
All	16%	78%	6%
Republicans	25%	70%	5%
Democrats	12%	85%	3%
Independents	14%	78%	8%

Taken from: CBS News/*New York Times* Poll, November 18–21, 2004.

What is this but allowing people to ignore conscience without consequence? Protecting people from the impact of public disapproval eliminates one of the most important social tools for imparting and shaping morals.

Moreover, using government to impose a conscienceless amorality on everyone threatens a true culture war. Goodman gets it entirely wrong when she writes: "the plea to protect their conscience is a thinly veiled ploy for conquest."

A legal prohibition on contraception would be an attempt at "conquest." Simply saying "I opt out, but I won't stop others" seeks to preserve social harmony in a diverse and free society.

Otherwise, there is no middle ground for coexistence: whatever government decides determines everyone's behavior. Everyone then has an added incentive to seize power and impose their beliefs on others.

The best strategy is to leave government rule-making at a minimum, limited to important issues which only government can decide. Then, as Goodman suggests, "what holds us together is the other lowly virtue, minding your own business."

Open markets allow even disagreeable people who disagree to live with a minimum of confrontation. A Chicago Planned Parenthood official argued: "A pharmacist's personal views cannot intrude on the relationship between a woman and her doctor."

They don't. The woman can fill her prescription elsewhere.

The refusal of any one doctor or pharmacist might be inconvenient to the customer involved. But there are more than 16,000 hospitals and 51,000 retail pharmacies across America.

Government could increase access to contraceptives by relaxing prescription requirements. In such a system everyone is able to choose. And everyone bears the cost of his or her choice.

Judy Waxman of the National Women's Law Center charges that the refusal to fill prescriptions is "based on personal beliefs, not on legitimate medical or professional concerns." But the same could be said of a person desiring contraceptives or an abortion.

The belief that such products or procedures are legitimate is intrinsically no more valid than the belief that they are illegitimate. Surely the moral views of medical professionals should be respected by people who emphasize the importance of "choice" and "controlling one's own body."

Unfortunately, the issue is generating widespread political battle. But public officials should remember the virtues of neutrality.

The best way to avoid social conflict is to respect everyone's conscience whenever possible. That's what free choice should mean in a liberal democracy like our own.

EVALUATING THE AUTHOR'S ARGUMENTS:

The author of this viewpoint often cites the opposition's point of view throughout his article. What do you think this does for his argument? Does the presentation of the opposition's perspective strengthen the author's, or does it weaken it? Explain your reasoning.

Pharmacists Should Not Be Allowed to Fill Birth Control Prescriptions

Dan K. Thomasson

"Those who seek a right to dispense pharmaceuticals should never be allowed to pick and choose which prescriptions they honor."

In the following viewpoint Dan K. Thomasson argues that pharmacists should be required to fill all prescriptions, including those for birth control. It is unethical for pharmacists to impose their beliefs and judgments on others, argues Thomasson, and certainly not their right to decide whether a woman should use birth control. Sometimes women need birth control because their health would be severely threatened if they were to become pregnant; other women may need emergency contraception to avoid becoming pregnant as a result of rape or incest. But regardless of the reason, Thomasson argues it is never alright to impose one's belief on others, especially when their health is at stake. For all of these reasons, Thomasson concludes that phar-

Dan K. Thomasson, "Birth-Control Denial the Height of Arrogance," *Seattle Post-Intelligencer,* July 14, 2008. Reproduced by permission of the author.

macists should fill all prescriptions that come their way without passing judgment on patients.

Dan K. Thomasson is a syndicated columnist and a former editor for the Scripps Howard News Service, a Washington, DC, news organization.

AS YOU READ, CONSIDER THE FOLLOWING QUESTIONS:
1. Why is it hypocritical for a pharmacist to deny a prescription for birth control but fill one for Viagra, according to the author?
2. What four states does the author say have passed laws mandating that pharmacies fill all prescriptions or help customers get them filled elsewhere?
3. According to the author, when is a "pharmacy not a pharmacy" and a "pharmacist not a pharmacist"?

A rape victim walks into a pharmacy with a prescription for a morning-after pill that will terminate a possible pregnancy and is told politely it will not be filled, and that she must go elsewhere, no matter how inconvenient. That is, if the pharmacist has the decency even to return the prescription.

The message is clear: Tough luck. If a child has been conceived in the violation of her body, it is the victim's sacred duty to have the baby.

Another woman, whose body will not support a pregnancy, submits a prescription for simple birth control pills and is also rejected. Or a young man and woman in the throes of hormonal conflict seek a package of condoms but can't purchase one, and then end up victims of normal, post-pubescent passion.

Are those and other examples exaggerations? Hardly. They are manifestations of a real effort by a growing movement of political- and religious-based groups to withhold access to birth control and anti-abortion measures through pharmaceutical denial.

Pharmacists Should Be Obligated to Fill All Prescriptions
So when is a pharmacy not a pharmacy? Better yet, when can a licensed pharmacist not fill a legitimate prescription because of political or

religious reasons? Should a state licensing authority permit the dispensing of male-enhancement drugs but not those that permit a female to guard her own health? Doesn't a licensed pharmacist have an implied contractual obligation to honor all verifiable prescriptions from practicing physicians?

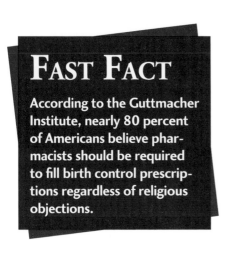

FAST FACT

According to the Guttmacher Institute, nearly 80 percent of Americans believe pharmacists should be required to fill birth control prescriptions regardless of religious objections.

Those are health, ethical and legal questions that most state authorities now find themselves facing with a growing number of pharmacists who refuse to honor prescribed contraceptives or sell those available over the counter on grounds it violates their consciences. Drugstores run by those who harbor strict beliefs about social issues are becoming more frequent, encouraged mainly by institutions—many religious based—that oppose any form of unnatural interference with pregnancy, be it wanted or not.

On the other hand, it seems, prescriptions for recently developed drugs that alleviate male dysfunction are no problem. Selling mechanical devices that do the same things as the "little blue pills" [Viagra and other male-enhancement drugs] presumably is also acceptable. It is all right, then, to encourage male participation in a healthy sex life but not the woman's right to protect herself from unwanted conditions.

Moral Righteousness Has No Place in Business

Realizing that I am about to bring down the wrath of those who see themselves as ordained guardians of our morals, I'm going to say it anyway:

What unmitigated arrogance! This kind of sanctimony has no place in a regulated and necessary business. Those who seek a right to dispense pharmaceuticals should never be allowed to pick and choose which prescriptions they honor based on extraneous considerations such as religious convictions or mere assertions that it violates their own personal codes.

Whether they disapprove of the drug on moral grounds is completely beside the point. They should follow the doctor's orders unless they suspect some irregularity, and that is that. If they can't agree with that, they should find another profession.

The Law Should Require Pharmacists to Fill Birth Control Prescriptions

It will be up to the states to determine how far they will let this abrogation of responsibility proceed. Several states—California, New Jersey, Illinois and Washington—already have passed laws requiring a pharmacy to fill all prescriptions or help women get them elsewhere.

(Editor's note: Lawyers representing Washington asked a federal appeals court last week [July 2008] to reinstate rules requiring pharmacists to dispense "morning-after" birth control pills. Last fall [2007], a federal judge in Seattle issued a preliminary injunction allowing pharmacists to refuse to sell the pill, but only if they refer customers to a nearby source.)

Boxes of Postinor-2 or the "morning after" pill sit in a pharmacy. The author argues that pharmacists should not be allowed to refuse to dispense birth control because of personal objections.

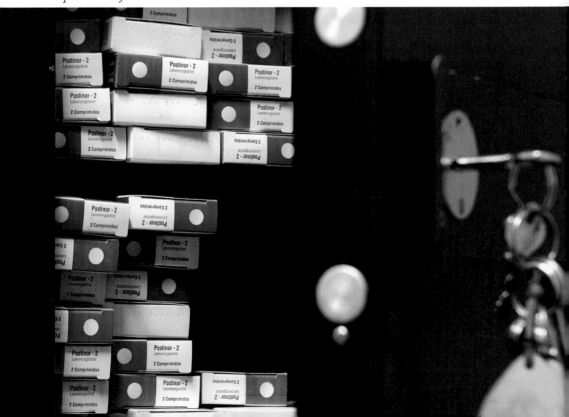

Ten other states reportedly are considering the same legislation. Some pro-choice groups and those who regard conscience-based pharmacies as a threat to the health and welfare of the nation are fighting it.

Fortunately, the major drugstore chains are not likely to follow this pattern and the scope will be limited to those stores sponsored by right to life groups. This may be a serious problem in rural areas, even if they say they will help women get what they need someplace else, which seems contradictory to their mission.

Personal Convictions Should Not Interfere with Professional Responsibility

It's all part of a sad trend to establish a strict religious-based social order, even in the health fields. Fertility doctors reportedly have refused to inseminate gay women and anesthesiologists have declined to participate in sterilization procedures such as vasectomies.

Personal convictions are fine unless they interfere with professional responsibility, especially when it pertains to treatments we don't endorse but that have been scientifically vetted as safe and legally prescribed. When that is denied, a pharmacy is not a pharmacy and a pharmacist not a pharmacist.

Would a Christian Scientist, who doesn't believe in doctors, refuse to put a tourniquet on the leg of a man who would bleed to death without it?

EVALUATING THE AUTHORS' ARGUMENTS:

In the previous viewpoint, Doug Bandow argued that if a woman encountered a pharmacist who did not want to fill her birth control prescription, she could just find another pharmacist who would. How do you think Dan K. Thomasson would respond to this argument? Use evidence from the texts in your answer.

Insurance Companies Should Cover the Cost of Birth Control Prescriptions

National Women's Law Center

"An employer's failure to provide insurance coverage for prescription contraceptives, when it covers other prescription drugs, devices, and preventive care, constitutes unlawful sex discrimination."

In the following viewpoint the National Women's Law Center argues that insurance companies should cover the cost of prescription birth control. Avoiding pregnancy is a critical concern for many women in the United States, the author explains. Unplanned pregnancies can have severe consequences, such as physical and emotional stress, as well as financial hardship. As such, a woman should have the right to decide if and when she gets pregnant. Excluding prescription contraceptives from health coverage plans, in the author's opinion, is unfair and inappropriate. Not covering birth control discriminates against women and puts them at a financial disadvantage, because they have to pay for the birth control themselves. This is even more unfair, considering

National Women's Law Center, "Coverage of Contraceptives in Health Insurance: The Facts You Should Know," www.nwlc.org, May 2008. Reproduced by permission.

that insurance companies often cover male enhancement medications such as Viagra. The National Women's Law Center concludes that if insurance plans cover other prescription drugs, they should also cover birth control.

Founded in 1972, the National Women's Law Center serves women and girls, especially those from low-income families. It aims to protect women's rights by arguing in support of new laws that benefit women, litigating cases on behalf of women in state and federal courts as well as the Supreme Court, and educating the public about laws that affect women and their families.

AS YOU READ, CONSIDER THE FOLLOWING QUESTIONS:
1. According to the author, why is access to contraception critical for women?
2. How does excluding prescription contraceptives from health insurance coverage unfairly disadvantage women, according to the author?
3. Who is Robyn Llewellyn, and how does she factor into the author's argument?

*T*wenty-four states have passed laws that require insurance companies to cover prescription contraceptives if they cover other prescription drugs. . . .

Why Women Need Insurance Coverage for Contraceptives
- Pregnancy prevention is central to good health care for women. Most women have the potential to become pregnant for over 30 years of their lives, and for approximately three-quarters of her reproductive life, the average woman is trying to postpone or avoid pregnancy.
- Access to contraception is critical to preventing unintended pregnancies and to enabling women to control the timing and spacing of their pregnancies, which in turn reduces the incidence of maternal death, low birth weight babies, and infant mortality.
- The exclusion of prescription contraceptives from health insurance coverage unfairly disadvantages women by singling out for

unfavorable treatment a health insurance need that only they have. Failure to cover contraception forces women to bear higher health care costs to avoid pregnancy, and exposes women to the unique physical, economic, and emotional consequences that can result from unintended pregnancy.

• One of the most immediate economic consequences of not providing contraceptive health coverage for women is the out-of-pocket cost of paying for contraception. Women insured through employer-sponsored insurance or with an individual policy are more likely than men to spend more than 10 percent of their income on out-of-pocket costs and premiums. . . .

Americans Support Contraceptive Coverage

A 2007 poll found that Americans think birth control should be covered more than memory drugs, in vitro fertilization, Viagra, weight-loss drugs, and other medications.

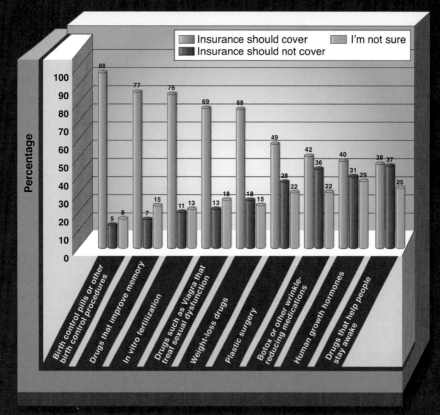

Taken from: Harris Poll, April 30, 2007.

Fighting for Contraception Coverage

- The ability of women to receive the contraceptive coverage they deserve has advanced significantly as a result of two interpretations of the federal civil rights laws, one by the Equal Employment Opportunity Commission (EEOC) and one by a federal court.
- In late 2000, the EEOC ruled that an employer's failure to provide insurance coverage for prescription contraceptives, when it covers other prescription drugs, devices, and preventive care, constitutes unlawful sex discrimination under Title VII of the Civil Rights Act of 1964. The National Women's Law Center led a coalition of 60 health care, women's, civil rights, and other groups asking the EEOC for such a ruling.
- The EEOC's ruling was followed by the 2001 decision, *Erickson v. Bartell Drug Co.*, in which the U.S. District Court for the Western District of Washington ruled that the defendant's exclusion of prescription contraceptives from its otherwise comprehensive employee health benefits plan constituted a violation of Title VII. The court's decision was the first one ever to rule definitively on the merits of this issue. The court, as a result, ordered Bartell Drug Co., the defendant, to cover each of the available options for prescription contraception to the same extent, and on the same terms, that it covers other drugs, devices, and preventive care for its employees, as well as all contraception-related outpatient services. The National Women's Law Center was part of the legal team representing the plaintiff in the class action lawsuit.

Fast Fact

A 2007 Harris Poll found that 81 percent of adults believe that insurance companies should cover the cost of birth control prescriptions.

- Unfortunately, the advances made in women's ability to gain contraceptive coverage under Title VII suffered a setback in March 2007. A divided panel of the Eighth Circuit Court of Appeals, under the particular factual circumstances in the case, held that the failure of Union Pacific Railroad to provide contraceptive coverage to its employees was not sex discrimination under federal law. The court determined that because Union Pacific excluded coverage for all contraceptives (prescription and non-prescription), and did not cover sterilization procedures for either men or women, insurance coverage was equal for men and women. In our view, this decision is in error and reflects a basic misunderstanding of the fundamental principles of discrimination. Fortunately for the women involved, Union Pacific changed its plan to include prescription contraceptives and has announced that it will not take away the coverage following the Eighth Circuit's decision.

Workers Demand Contraceptive Coverage

- On January 1, 2007, Wal-Mart, the nation's largest private sector employer, began offering contraceptive coverage to its employees. This victory was achieved after five years of litigation. In October 2002, Wal-Mart employee Lisa Smith Mauldin of Dallas, Georgia filed a sex discrimination class action lawsuit against Wal-Mart because it did not cover her birth control pills. The National Women's Law Center was part of Mauldin's legal team. As a result of Wal-Mart's decision, the case was voluntarily dismissed.

- In 2006, after pressure from a local coalition working with the National Women's Law Center, the State of Wyoming health insurance plan was amended to include contraceptive coverage, as the vast majority of states already do.

- In February 2006, Robin Llewellyn, a Seattle resident who is a licensed third mate in the Merchant Marine, urged her health plan, the Masters, Mates & Pilots (MM&P) Plan, to add contraceptives to its prescription drug package. MM&P covers over 70 employers in the maritime shipping industry, providing health insurance to thousands of beneficiaries. When the plan refused to add contraceptive coverage, the National Women's Law Center wrote on Ms. Llewellyn's behalf advising it of the legal requirements and demanding the addition of this coverage. MM&P then promptly added the coverage.

- In December 2003, the National Women's Law Center intervened on behalf of an employee of a newspaper publisher in Michigan— Independent Newspapers, Inc.—and persuaded the company to add contraceptive coverage to its health plan.

- A Lenox Hill Hospital employee in New York City contacted the National Women's Law Center in spring 2003 because the hospital did not include oral contraceptives in its prescription drug plan. The

After five years of litigation, in January 2007 Wal-Mart began offering contraceptive coverage for its employees.

National Women's Law Center wrote to the hospital and hospital officials quickly agreed to add this coverage.

- In spring 2003, the National Women's Law Center was successful in working with the American Federation of State, County, and Municipal Employees (AFSCME) to secure contraceptive coverage for the employees of the city of Eugene, Oregon.
- Daimler-Chrysler joined automakers Ford and General Motors in adding contraceptive coverage in June 2002.
- In December 2002, Dow Jones and Company agreed to provide coverage for all FDA-approved prescription contraceptives and related medical services in all of its health plans for its employees,

as part of a settlement of charges that had been filed with the EEOC by employees and their union.

- In April 2001, at the University of Nebraska, several female faculty and staff members urged the University administration to add contraceptive coverage—with legal assistance from the National Women's Law Center—and the University regents agreed.

EVALUATING THE AUTHOR'S ARGUMENTS:

The National Women's Law Center argues that health insurance plans that do not cover the cost of prescription birth control discriminate against women. Clarify what the author means by this. Do you agree? Explain your answer thoroughly.

Viewpoint
4

Insurance Companies Should Not Cover the Cost of Birth Control Prescriptions

"The pill does not qualify as a legitimate treatment for an ailment and therefore should not be covered by health insurance."

Judie Brown

In the following viewpoint Judie Brown argues that birth control prescriptions should not be covered by health insurance. Birth control pills are used to prevent pregnancy, she explains, and thus do not qualify as a medical treatment. The pill was created to give women freedom from sexual accountability and does not serve to protect women from disease or treat a medical condition. Furthermore, Brown views the fact that emergency contraceptives are used to terminate pregnancies as immoral, and she believes they are not worthy of being paid for by insurance plans. Brown concludes that health care plans should be used to cover the costs of

Judie Brown, "If It Looks Like Birth Control, It Probably Is!" American Life League, July 11, 2008. Reproduced by permission.

treating disease and other medical conditions—not for potentially ending a human life.

Judie Brown is president and cofounder of American Life League, the nation's largest grassroots pro-life educational organization. She is also currently serving her second five-year term as a member of the Pontifical Academy for Life in Rome.

AS YOU READ, CONSIDER THE FOLLOWING QUESTIONS:
1. In Brown's opinion, why should insurance companies cover Viagra but not the birth control pill?
2. According to the author, birth control pills were created for what purpose? Why does she think this means they should be ineligible for coverage?
3. What three consequences does the author say could result from taking oral contraceptives?

The recent debate in the media over whether or not Viagra has the same status for health insurance purposes as the birth control pill is an interesting one. The real question to ask is whether the pill is actually needed for medicating a treatable condition. The very fact that the question has arisen gives pause to examine another type of debate, which is actually fundamental to our vision of the human person.

Birth Control Pills Do Not Treat Disease

When Viagra came on the scene ten years ago, the alleged physical condition for which the pill would be used as treatment was something known as erectile dysfunction, also known as impotence, which is a condition that does affect a large number of men. The medication became controversial not so much because it existed but because the television ads were offensive to certain groups of people. Be that as it may, the medicine has a role to play in the treatment of men according to many medical professionals.

So how does this pill, which is a valid medical treatment, compare to the birth control pill, which does not treat a disease or medical condition?

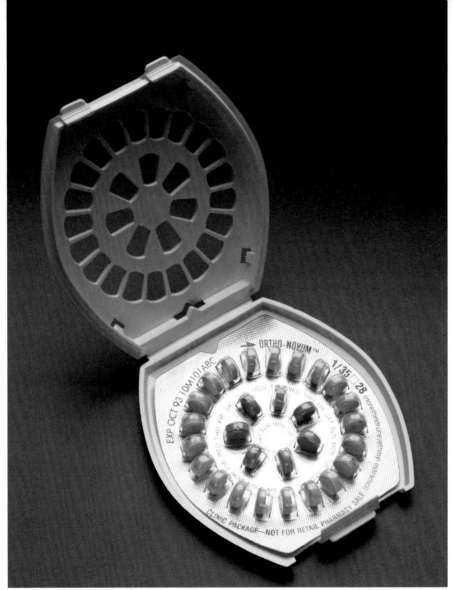

Because birth control pills do not treat a disease or a medical condition, many feel they should not be covered by insurance.

Why should they have equal status when it comes to what health insurance coverage should provide?

Well, I cannot think of a comparison, and I am now compelled to tell you why.

"The Pill Was and Is a Recreational Drug"

When the birth control pill was first conceived in the mind of Dr. Gregory Pincus, an endocrinologist, the primary goal was to find some type of chemical that would inhibit the onset of pregnancy. That way, men and women would be free of the worry associated with the possibility of procreating a child and then having to accept responsibility for raising that child. Or, as one biographical sketch of Pincus states, "By creating the first practical oral contraceptive, the birth control pill, in the 1950s, Gregory Pincus brought privacy and convenience to women worldwide."

While the current debate would deny it, the fundamental fact is that indeed the pill was never devised to assist anyone in treating a disease or malfunction of the human body, but rather was created specifically to solve the perceived social problem of pregnancy by preventing it. Or, to put it another way, the pill was and is a recreational drug.

Sadly, in the intervening 50+ years, the pill has been through a number of public relations campaigns and the vast majority of the American public views it as a necessity today. Any citizen would be hard-pressed to tell you precisely why pregnancy has become classified as a medical condition similar to cancer or typhoid.

Obviously that is not what the pill is all about; it has never been a treatment but rather a marketable entity designed to guarantee freedom of sexual license without accountability. Or, as the Pincus biographical sketch opines, "The cultural impact of the pill is wide-reaching, allowing women the liberty of choosing a method of birth control that can be administered in the privacy of their own homes."

FAST FACT

Only twenty-four states require that insurance companies that have prescription plans include birth control in their coverage.

Health Insurance Should Not Cover Birth Control

So when a debate ensues that centers on the reasons why health insurance should cover both Viagra and the birth control pill, the obvious response is that the pill does not qualify as a legitimate treatment for an ailment and therefore should not be covered by health insurance.

• Viagra may treat impotence and thus help the sufferer recover bodily health.

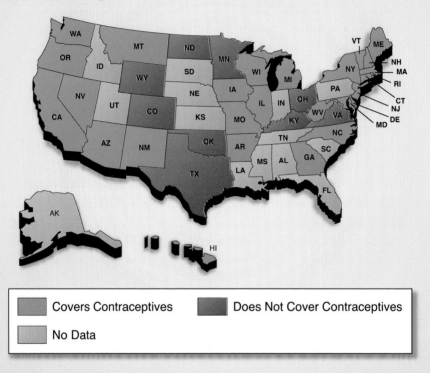

Insurance Coverage of Contraceptives

Birth control coverage is mixed in the United States. Twenty-seven states require insurers to cover contraceptives, but nine do not provide coverage.

Covers Contraceptives   Does Not Cover Contraceptives

No Data

Taken from: Guttmacher Institute, September 1, 2008.

- The pill will possibly prevent a female from getting pregnant, will not protect her from acquiring sexually transmitted disease, could contribute to her suffering from myriad health problems including cancer and heart disease and is generally an artificial pollutant of the human body.

In conclusion, it should be obvious that a company interested in insuring the continued health of an individual would never provide the means for that person to ingest a chemical that could make her sick and might kill a baby.

It is a no brainer—health insurance is all about preserving health and restoring health, not destroying it.

Chapter 3

What Restrictions Should Be Placed on Birth Control?

The debate over allowing teens unfettered access to birth control is one that covers several issues, including the legal rights of teens.

Teens Should Need Parental Consent to Get Birth Control

Harvard Crimson

"Would you want your 12-year-old coming home from middle school with birth control pills?"

In the following viewpoint the *Harvard Crimson* argues that teens should need their parents' permission to get birth control. The author discusses a case in which a Maine school board passed a measure that would allow middle school children to get birth control pills without requiring parental permission. Such a plan is both dangerous and careless, the author explains. Birth control pills can cause hormonal fluctuations that can be unsafe for young girls. It is in the interest of safety that parents should be aware of what medications their teens consume, the author claims. In addition, parents have the right to know about the sexual activity of their sons and daughters so they can provide them with appropriate information about sex. As legal guardians, it is a parent's responsibility to protect their children and help them make the best decisions possible, including whether to engage in sex or not. For all these reasons, the author concludes that teen access to birth control should require parental consent.

Founded in 1873, the *Harvard Crimson* is the nation's oldest continuously published daily college newspaper. It is located on the Harvard campus in Cambridge, Massachusetts, and staffed by undergraduate volunteers.

AS YOU READ, CONSIDER THE FOLLOWING QUESTIONS:
1. According to the author, what reason did officials from the Portland, Maine, middle school give for why it distributed birth control pills to students?
2. Whose trust did the middle school health officials betray when they provided students with birth control pills, according to the author?
3. What action does the author suggest schools take when students require contraceptives?

Would you want your 12-year-old child coming home from middle school with birth control pills?

Careless and Inappropriate

Strange as it may seem, that is a question that some residents of Portland, Maine will have to wrestle with after the school board last week [October 2007] passed a measure allowing an independently-run clinic at a local middle school to distribute prescription-strength birth control pills without parental permission. Any student wishing to receive the pills will have to undergo counseling and be examined by a physician or nurse who can prescribe the drugs. And parents do have to sign a waiver to give their children access to any of the clinic's services. But the decision to prescribe the pill without notifying parents has sent shockwaves through the local community and garnered the attention of the national press.

Local health officials told *The New York Times* that the decision was made to distribute the pill at the middle school in light of the fact that 17 students there have become pregnant in the past few years.

Their argument was that if a small minority of the school is sexually active, the school should provide the resources to all, regardless of their age, to protect that minority. Although these circumstances may have precipitated the need for such a measure, providing the pill to middle school students without parental permission is nonetheless inappropriate and contradictory to the purpose of public schools in the United States.

Not the Responsibility of Public Schools

A school is meant to serve as a surrogate guardian of students during the school day while students' parents are at work, but this policy works to undermine the authority of the parents. By allowing these teen and pre-teen students to receive these contraceptives—which can cause hormone levels to fluctuate and facilitate unprotected sexual contact—the school is in practice betraying the trust placed in it by the parents of its students. While this action would be permissible in a private school, the fact that the school where this program is being enacted is public makes it objectionable, because taxpayer dollars are being used to fund it.

Middle school students fall between the ages of 12 and 15, an age where peer pressure can cause students to do things they later regret. While it has not been shown that easy access to birth control increases sexual activity among students, it certainly doesn't deter them or require them to carefully consider their

FAST FACT

According to the Heritage Foundation, two-thirds of teenagers share their parents' beliefs about sex.

options. Instead of dispensing these pills, the school should focus on a comprehensive sexual education curriculum that informs the students of the risks involved with sexual activity as well as the side effects of birth control. If a school district decides that it is absolutely necessary that it provide guidance and assistance to students who require contraception, it should give them information about outside organizations, such as Planned Parenthood, that could help rather than giving the pill to students directly.

Texas governor Rick Perry signs the Abortion Consent Bill, which requires parental consent for a minor to get an abortion. The author argues that parents should be informed of their children's sexual activity especially when medical treatment is involved.

Some may argue that parents sign a waiver that describes the services rendered by the clinic before their child can access it. But by pairing the distribution of contraception with access to quality medical care, the school board is forcing parents to make a cruel all-or-nothing choice.

Schools Should Focus on Sex Education

In an age in which teens are becoming more sexually active at younger ages, it is important that our schools educate them about alternative options while still protecting those students who do choose to have sex. Though weighing the balance between protecting students and betraying parents can be difficult, this program clearly comes down on the side of the latter. Instead, the school should focus on education and providing access to outside resources, and leave the dispensing of free birth control to someone else.

EVALUATING THE AUTHOR'S ARGUMENTS:

In the viewpoint you just read, the author argues that public schools should not dispense birth control to students without parental consent. What do you think? Do you think schools violate parents' trust by giving students birth control? Or do you think the main goal of a school is to serve its students' needs? Explain your position.

Teens Should Not Need Parental Consent to Get Birth Control

Center for Reproductive Rights

"Minors have a right to privacy that includes their ability to use contraception."

In the following viewpoint the Center for Reproductive Rights argues that teens should be allowed to get birth control without the consent of their parents. The author opposes regulations that would require teens to obtain parental consent to buy condoms, get birth control, or request emergency contraception from a pharmacy. The author warns that requiring parental consent will actually encourage teens to have unprotected sex—many teens would opt not to use birth control rather than tell their parents they are sexually active. As a result, teens would be more likely to get pregnant and contract an STD. The author argues that all teens have a constitutional right to privacy—forcing them to ask their parents' permission to use birth control violates that right. Because privacy is a fundamental right for all Americans, the author con-

Center for Reproductive Rights, "Parental Consent and Notice for Contraceptives Threatens Teen Health and Constitutional Rights," reproductiverights.org, November 2006. Reproduced by permission.

cludes that teens should be allowed to obtain contraception without the consent of their parents.

The Center for Reproductive Rights is an organization that seeks to protect women's reproductive rights. The Center uses the law to advance women's choice about when to have children and supports programs that provide women with the best reproductive health care available in the United States and throughout the world.

AS YOU READ, CONSIDER THE FOLLOWING QUESTIONS:
1. According to the author, what two federal programs protect teens' privacy regarding contraception?
2. According to the author, what threat does parental consent pose to teens' health and well-being?
3. What did the Supreme Court say in 1977 about birth control, as reported by the author?

Currently, no state or federal laws require minors to get parental consent in order to get contraception. Increasingly, however, proposals are being introduced to restrict teens' access to reproductive health care by calling for parental consent or notification.

Mandatory Parental Consent Hurts Some Teens
Teens in a variety of circumstances would be affected if required to obtain parental consent for contraception:

- A young woman seeking contraception from a clinic—birth control pills, DepoProvera, diaphragm—would be forced to obtain parental permission
- A minor who buys condoms at a pharmacy could be turned away without parental consent
- A teen who seeks emergency contraception because of forced or unanticipated intercourse would need approval, even though emergency contraception must be used within 72 hours of unprotected intercourse.

Two Types of Parental Consent

- Mandatory parental consent would force teenagers to get permission from one or two parents before getting contraception.
- Mandatory parental notification would require young people to tell one or two parents about their plans to get contraception. Mandatory notification poses the same danger of discouraging contraceptive use by teens as does the requirement of consent. If a minor is fearful about discussing contraception with a parent, there is no difference between "telling" the parent and getting parental permission.

Federal Programs Protect Confidentiality for Teens

Two federal programs—Title X and Medicaid—protect teens' privacy and prohibit parental consent requirements for teens seeking contraception. Title X provides funds to states for family planning services; Medicaid covers health care services for low-income women. Both programs mandate that, in exchange for receiving monies from the federal government, health care services treat all patients confidentially, including teens.

Attempts by states to implement parental consent requirements for contraceptive services that are funded by these programs have

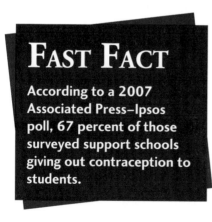

FAST FACT

According to a 2007 Associated Press–Ipsos poll, 67 percent of those surveyed support schools giving out contraception to students.

been invalidated when challenged in court. Courts find that the requirements impermissibly conflict with federal program requirements. Federal program rules mandating confidentiality preempt state efforts to make new requirements. Nevertheless, states have continued to introduce legislation that would mandate parental involvement in teens' private contraceptive decisions.

Parental contact requirements discourage teens from seeking contraception, even though they may already be sexually active. Confidentiality can be a determining factor for teens deciding whether or not to seek contraceptive protection.

Parents' Beliefs About Consequences of Parental Notification Laws for Contraception

Parents think there are more negatives than positives to requiring teens to get their parents' permission for birth control. While they think requiring teens to get parental permission will help kids think before having sex and talk to their parents, more believe such laws would encourage teens to have unprotected sex.

	Consequences	Yes	No	Do Not Know/ Refused
Negative	Use nonclinic birth control methods	75.5%	18.3%	6.2%
	More unprotected sex	67.3%	25.5%	7.2%
	More pregnancies	58.5%	32.4%	9.1%
	More STDs	58.2%	30.8%	11.0%
	Stop/delay getting birth control	56.2%	35.2%	8.6%
	Stop going to clinics	48.0%	43.6%	8.4%
	Travel out of state to get birth control	46.2%	47.0%	6.8%
Positive	Think more before sex	42.2%	51.4%	6.4%
	Talk more with parents	33.1%	58.5%	8.4%
	Have less sex	15.4%	79.1%	5.6%
	Stop having sex	3.6%	94.3%	2.2%

Taken from: Marla E. Eisenburg et al., "Parental Notification Laws for Minors' Access to Contraception: What Do Parents Say?" *Archives of Pediatrics and Adolescent Medicine*, February 2005, p. 124.

Teenagers Need Access to Contraceptive Services

Almost half of women in the United States have intercourse by the time that they turn 18. While the teen pregnancy rate today has dropped slightly in the past twenty years, almost one million teens become pregnant each year. A sexually active teen using no contraception has a 90% chance of becoming pregnant within a one year period, according to the Alan Guttmacher Institute.

Lack of contraception increases the chances of unintended pregnancy. Nearly 80% of teen pregnancies are unplanned in the U.S. Teen pregnancy rates are much higher in the U.S. than in other industrial countries—double the rates in England; nine times as high as the Netherlands. Lack of contraception also increases the possibility of exposure to sexually transmitted diseases. About three million U.S. teens acquire a sexually transmitted infection every year.

Parental Consent Laws Threaten Teens' Health

Supporters of measures forcing teens to notify or get consent from their parents argue that they promote the best interests of young women and improve family communications.

These arguments are out of touch with reality. These proposed laws threaten adolescent health and well-being. Even teens who could comply with parental consent requirements will face delays in getting contraceptive services. Additional clinic visits, missed school or work time, and increased expense will result.

Many young women live in nontraditional situations—with one parent, a stepparent, other relatives, or on their own. Contact with biological parents, if required by law, may be impossible.

Some teens face violence or other severe consequences from parents as a result of informing their parents that they are seeking contraceptive services. Minors fearful of retribution may forgo using contraception altogether, even though they are already sexually active.

Teens who seek contraceptive services are generally sexually active already. They benefit from meeting with health care providers, who can provide screening, counseling about sexually transmitted diseases, and education about other reproductive health concerns. . . .

Parental Consent for Contraception Is Unconstitutional

Minors have a right to privacy that includes their ability to use contraception.

The U.S. Supreme Court said in 1977 that denial of contraception is not a permissible way to deter sexual activity.

Courts that have addressed attempts to impose parental consent or notification requirements have found that these types of laws conflict with a minor's constitutional right to privacy.

Although states may require parental consent for a minor's abortion when sufficient alternatives, such as judicial bypass, are in place, the same reasoning does not apply to contraception. According to the U.S. Supreme Court, "The states' interest in protection of the mental and physical health of the pregnant minor, and in protection of potential life are clearly more implicated by the abortion decision than by the decision to use a nonhazardous contraceptive."

Access to contraceptive services is considered a fundamental privacy right and has remained so for over three decades.

Bad Policy Endangers Teen Lives

Placing barriers on teen access to contraception is dangerous to the health and welfare of young women because it increases their risk of unplanned pregnancies. The costs to society from teen pregnancy are enormous.

By allowing teens unconstrained access to birth control the author feels teens are more likely to practice safe sex.

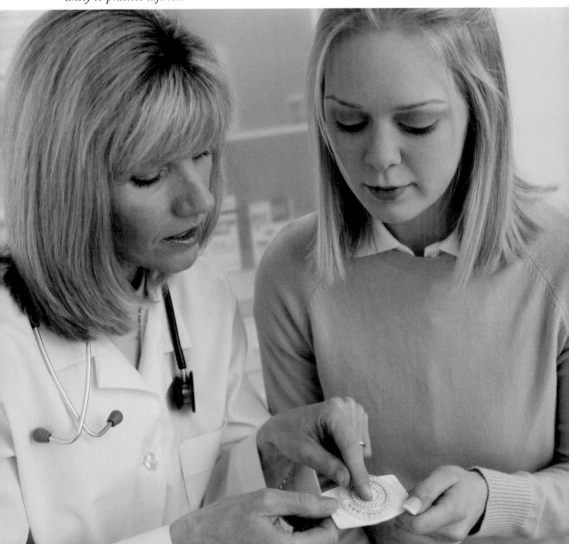

While programs with federal family planning money are forbidden from requiring parental consent or notice for teen services, teens also have a constitutional right to privacy that encompasses their decision to obtain contraception, a right that lawmakers should acknowledge and respect.

EVALUATING THE AUTHOR'S ARGUMENTS:

In the viewpoint you read, the author suggests that requiring teens to obtain parental consent for contraception is unconstitutional. At what age do you think teens should be allowed to get birth control? Do parents deserve a say in their children's personal sex lives? Why or why not? Explain your position.

Teens Should Be Allowed Over-the-Counter Access to Emergency Contraception

"Eliminating barriers to both routine and emergency contraception is imperative to preventing teen pregnancy and abortion in the U.S."

D.C. Weiss, C.C. Harper, J.J. Speidel, and T.R. Raine

In the following viewpoint the authors for the Bixby Center for Global Reproductive Health argue that teens should be given access to over-the-counter emergency contraception (EC). EC, a hormonal contraceptive that can be taken within seventy-two hours after unprotected sex, greatly reduces a woman's chance of becoming pregnant. Each year in the United States there are nearly 1 million teen pregnancies, so teens need as much help as possible accessing EC to help them avoid getting pregnant, according to the authors. The authors argue that accessing EC does not threaten teen health or cause a rise in sexual activity—it merely helps those teens who have had sex prevent pregnancy in the event the condom they used broke. Many

D.C. Weiss, C.C. Harper, J.J. Speidel, and T.R. Raine, "Should Teens Be Denied Equal Access to Emergency Contraception?" Bixby Center for Global Reproductive Health, 2008. Reproduced by permission.

unwanted pregnancies can be prevented if teens are allowed over-the-counter access to emergency contraceptives, the authors conclude.

Formed in 1999 at the University of California at San Francisco, the Bixby Center for Global Reproductive Health works to advance new reproductive health technologies, including birth control, while addressing the health, social, and economic consequences of sex and reproduction.

AS YOU READ, CONSIDER THE FOLLOWING QUESTIONS:

1. According to the authors, what effect do giving information on EC to fourteen- to fifteen-year-olds have on their sexual activity?
2. What percent of high school–based health centers do the authors say provide EC prescriptions for students?
3. How many sexually active teens do the authors say would not use birth control at all if they were required to get parental consent to do so?

Teenagers often lack adequate knowledge about pregnancy prevention: one-third of male and female teens report that they did not receive formal education on birth control, and two-thirds of males and one-half of females did not talk to a parent about contraception before age 18. Additionally, many sexually active teens do not use contraception or use less effective methods. Among 15–19-year-olds, 26 percent of females and 18 percent of males did not use any method of contraception the first time they had sex. The most popular method of contraception for teens is the condom, yet less than half (48 percent) of males and only 28 percent of females report using condoms every time they had sex over the course of one year. Despite these high rates of unprotected sex, only eight percent of teens have used emergency contraception (EC). Thus, there is a need for improved knowledge of and access to all methods of contraception.

EC Does Not Increase Sexual Activity

A substantial body of scientific evidence has demonstrated that there is no association between knowledge of and access to EC and sexual behavior of teens. For example, young teens (aged 14–15) who learn about EC in school are no more likely to become sexually active than their peers who do not receive such education. Further, teens and young women (aged 13–21) who have used EC in the past are not at increased risk for future pregnancies or sexually transmitted infections (STIs) compared to nonusers.

Perhaps more significantly, a number of advance provision studies have determined that enhancing access to EC does not increase teens' sexual or contraceptive risk-taking behaviors. Specifically, advance provision does not affect frequency of unprotected sex or use of condoms or birth control pills among teens. These findings have been corroborated by a study of teens and young women (aged 15–24), which also found that advance provision of EC does not increase number of

Some statistics show that the knowledge of emergency contraceptives such as Plan B do not actually increase or initiate sexual activity in teens, but they still remain widely unavailable as a form of birth control.

sexual partners or STI risk. Furthermore, even though participants in this study received multiple supplies of EC, they did not use it repeatedly in lieu of routine methods of contraception, nor did they report feeling increased pressure to have sex. However, teens who received EC in advance of need were more likely to use it when needed, and to take it within 12 hours after unprotected sex when it is most effective.

Teens Should Be Informed About EC

Despite the fact that EC has minimal side effects and no bearing on teenage sexual activity, its availability remains limited. Many doctors are not knowledgeable about EC and do not educate their patients about it: a survey of pediatricians in New York found that the majority (73 percent) could not identify any of the FDA-approved methods of EC, and only 17 percent regularly counseled their adolescent patients about its availability. Additionally, in a nationwide survey of high school–based health centers, 40 percent indicated that they did not offer education or referrals for EC, and only 30 percent provided EC prescriptions. . . .

One in five sexually active adolescents reported that they would use no contraception, or would use withdrawal, if parental notification was required to obtain prescription birth control. Nearly half would rely on a less effective, over-the-counter method such as condoms, which are more effective than withdrawal, but less effective than hormonal contraception. Similarly, a study of adolescents obtaining EC in Washington State—where it is available directly from a pharmacist for women of all ages—found that 22 percent would not use EC, but rather, would wait to see whether they got pregnant, if pharmacy access was not available. Thus, eliminating barriers to both routine and emergency contraception is imperative to preventing teen pregnancy and abortion in the U.S. . . .

FAST FACT

Emergency contraception is 75 to 94 percent effective in preventing pregnancy when taken within three days of having sex, according to the Society for Adolescent Medicine.

Having Access to Emergency Contraception (EC) Does Not Make Women More Promiscuous

Women who are given EC in advance have sex just as often, with as many partners, and use condoms and contract STDs at the same or similar rates as women who must go to a clinic to get it.

	Sexual Behavior	Women Given EC in Advance	Women Who Have Access to EC Through a Clinic
Frequency of sex	Never	3.0%	4.8%
	Less than 1 time per month	14.9%	14.2%
	1–3 times per month	26.4%	27.1%
	1 time per week	22.8%	22.3%
	More than 1 time per week	32.9%	31.6%
Number of sex partners	None	3.0%	4.8%
	1	75.2%	76.1%
	2	15.4%	11.9%
	3 or more	6.4%	7.1%
Frequency of condom use	Every time	21.2%	21.4%
	Most of the time	23.3%	24.6%
	Some of the time	24.2%	23.0%
	Never	28.3%	26.2%
	No intercourse	3.0%	4.8%
STD test results	Positive for chlamydia	2.3%	1.4%
	Positive for herpes	4.4%	4.8%

Taken from: Bixby Center for Global Reproductive Health, 2008.

Teens Will Benefit from Access to EC

Of the 840,000 teen pregnancies in the U.S. each year, more than 80 percent are unintended, and 40 percent of these end in abortion. The U.S. teen birth rate is higher than that of any other developed country, including Canada (two times higher), Germany (four times higher), France (five times higher), and Japan (nearly nine times higher). Teenagers are a vulnerable population that face a host of barriers to accessing family planning services and therefore stand much to gain from improved knowledge of and access to all methods of contraception. EC offers a safe and effective back-up method of birth control and does not adversely affect teens' sexual behavior. There is no scientifically valid reason to restrict its access.

EVALUATING THE AUTHORS' ARGUMENTS:

Like the other authors in this chapter, the authors for the Bixby Center for Global Reproductive Health argue that teen pregnancy is a serious problem. Yet their solution to the problem is to give teens unfettered access to EC and other birth control methods, while other authors believe teaching about birth control increases the problem of teen pregnancy. In one or two sentences, explain each author's position on teen pregnancy and their proposed solution.

Over-the-Counter Access to Emergency Contraception Is Unsafe

Wendy Wright

"Easy access allows someone other than the consumer to buy it and then slip it to a woman without her knowledge or consent."

Emergency contraception (EC) should not be available without a prescription, argues Wendy Wright in the following viewpoint. If the morning-after pill (MAP) were able to be purchased over the counter, it would jeopardize women's health in three main ways. First, nonprescription MAPs could be bought by men who want to make sure the women they have sex with do not get pregnant. Wright warns they could slip it into a woman's—or an adolescent's—drink without her knowledge or consent. Secondly, Wright argues that the MAP has only been deemed safe for a few groups of women—yet making it available over the counter will give all women access to it. Finally, easy access to the MAP is likely to increase rates of STDs, because Wright believes that women would be less likely to have sex with a condom if they think the

Wendy Wright, "Talking Points on the Morning-After Pill (MAP): Why the Morning-After Pill Should Not Be Available Without a Prescription," Concerned Women for America (cwfa.org), 2006. Reproduced by permission.

MAP will protect them from getting pregnant. Wright concludes that restricting access to emergency contraception helps keep both women and teens safe and healthy.

Wendy Wright is president of Concerned Women for America, a women's public policy organization that promotes the principles contained within the Bible.

AS YOU READ, CONSIDER THE FOLLOWING QUESTIONS:
1. Who is Gary Bourgeois, and how does he factor into the author's argument?
2. Name three ways in which the author claims that morning-after pill proponents have misled the public on the safety of emergency contraception.
3. What effect does the morning-after pill have on teen sexuality, according to Wright?

The morning-after pill (MAP) lacks testing for safety to women. Access to the drug over-the-counter, or without a prescription, would prompt use among consumers who, unknowingly, have medical conditions that put them at high risk of life-threatening complications. It could be slipped to women without their knowledge, and statutory rapists would rely on it to cover up their abuse of adolescents. In areas that allow easy access, the sexually transmitted disease rates have skyrocketed. The drug owner encourages multiple sex partners (putting women at risk of sexually transmitted diseases, or STDs), and endorses frequent use of the drug, though it has not conducted studies on multiple use. Morning-after pill promoters have been found guilty of overstating the efficacy of the drug and understating the risks to women.

Potential Risks to Women

Over-the-counter access would extend the availability of the MAP to a broader population than any study has included—females who have not been counseled or screened for contraindications.

Easy access allows someone other than the consumer to buy it and then slip it to a woman without her knowledge or consent. Unlike other drugs like aspirin, there is more potential for abuse by someone who, contrary to or unaware of the woman's wishes, does not want her pregnant. Drugs less easy to administer have been used against women:

> In one example, Gary Bourgeois' girlfriend refused to have an abortion. During sexual relations, he inserted misoprostol, used in the RU-486 abortion regimen. Later she experienced violent cramps then felt a partly dissolved pill drop from her vagina. Her baby died. He pleaded guilty to aggravated assault and administering a noxious substance in Canada in September, 2003.
>
> In another incident, Dr. Stephen Pack pleaded guilty to injecting Joy Schepis with an abortion-inducing drug in April 2000. The Bronx, New York, doctor jabbed his former lover with a syringe filled with methotrexate, which causes abortions, because she refused to have one.

It will be difficult for doctors to treat complications when the woman's medical history is unknown or hidden.

Women Are Protected by Physician Oversight

The morning-after pill is a high dose of the birth control pill, which requires a medical exam, a prescription, and physician oversight. Birth control pills can cause significant or life-threatening conditions such as blood clots, stroke and heart attacks. Birth control pills are contraindicated for women with diabetes, liver problems, heart disease, breast cancer, deep vein thrombosis, and for women who smoke and are over 35. Physician oversight is necessary to ensure that none of these contraindications exists. For example, according to the Centers for Disease Control, approximately 1.85 million women of reproductive age (18–44) have diabetes; approximately 500,000 do not know that they have the disease.

The World Health Organization has warned: "There may be a higher percentage of ectopic pregnancies among emergency contraceptive pill failure cases than among a normal pregnant population."

Nurses at the Royal College of Nursing warned that pharmacists in the United Kingdom (where the drug is available behind the counter) were failing to warn customers of possible complications or carry out routine medical assessments.

There Is a Lot We Do Not Know

[There is a] lack or absence of scientific studies on:

- The long-term effects [of the morning-after pill].
- The high dosage. A drug's safety at one dose or range of doses does not mean that the drug is equally safe at a much higher dose. Yet proponents stake their arguments on decades of use of the birth control pill, a lower dose—which is not available over-the-counter.
- Repeated usage. In the United Kingdom, one in seven of all women used the morning-after pill repeatedly in the same year.
- Females not screened for medical contraindications.
- Adolescents.
- The Food and Drug Administration's approval of the morning-after pill with a prescription was not based on controlled scientific studies, but on unscientific, anecdotal evidence. All studies (including those cited in the over-the-counter approval application of Plan B, a brand of the MAP) focus on the drug's relative reliability in decreasing the expected birth rate, not on the effect on the women who have taken the drug regimen.

Reasons Not to Trust Morning-After Pill Proponents

The FDA found Plan B's promoters guilty of false advertising, for overstating efficacy (claiming greater effectiveness in prohibiting pregnancies than the evidence shows) and understating the medical risks to women. The FDA stated the "ads raise significant public health and safety concerns." Yet proponents continue to make similar claims.

Plan B's promoters make the contradictory claim that the MAP inhibits implantation but does not end a pregnancy. Nearly half of Americans (46 percent) believe life begins at fertilization. Knowledge that the MAP can terminate a pregnancy could affect a woman's decision to use it; withholding such information violates the principle of informed consent.

Promoters have relied on junk science to claim it does not affect sexual behaviors. At least one study (from the University of Pittsburgh) included only teenagers already engaged in risky sexual activity, and then concluded that easy access to MAP did not change their behavior.

The American College of Obstetricians and Gynecologists (ACOG) recommends that low-dose oral contraceptives be available only with a prescription from a licensed health-care provider. Yet it is recommending that Plan B and other higher-dose hormone regimens be available over-the-counter.

ACOG did not poll its members. Its recommendation is not representative of its members. MAP proponents had complained that doctors have not been willing to hand out the drug to anyone (apparently a driving reason for them to seek over-the-counter status—to bypass medical intervention intended to protect women).

FAST FACT

Only 8 percent of sexually active teens have used emergency contraception, according to the Bixby Center for Global Reproductive Health.

A Disturbing Lack of Concern

MAP promoters demonstrate a disturbing lack of concern for women's health:

> Plan B's Web site responds to the question, "How often can Plan B be provided," by stating, "Plan B can be provided as frequently as needed."

> The Web site acknowledges the need for intervention and oversight. "Providers can help a client determine whether Plan B treatment makes sense given the timing of unprotected intercourse and her level of concern about an unwanted pregnancy." However, over-the-counter access would eliminate "providers," thereby eliminating the opportunity for counsel, caution, and the screening out of women with contraindications.

> The Web site encourages unnecessary use of the MAP for women already taking oral contraceptives—even though women are only fertile within days of ovulation: "Women taking oral contraception do not have true menstrual cycles and are at risk of pregnancy. . . . [E]mergency contraception may be indicated."

Advertisements for Plan B include:
- One ad portraying 13 young men with the caption, "So many men. So many reasons to have back up contraception."
- Another pictures a fraternity, with the words, "Delta Delta Thi. 27 upstanding young men. 34 billion sneaky little sperm."
- Another is designed like a poster for adolescents, describing "Damian" as "A Renaissance Guy, a Deep Thinker, an Ancient Soul, a Walking Sperm Factory."

Potential Effect on Public Health

Regions that allow easy access to the MAP experience a significant increase in sexually transmitted diseases. In the United Kingdom, chlamydia cases rose from 7,000 in 1999 to 10,000 cases [in 2005]. Gonorrhea cases climbed nearly 50 percent, to nearly 3,000 cases [in 2005], up from 2,000 in 1999. The highest increases were among 16–19 year olds.

Contrary to proponents' claims, the number of surgical abortions has not declined with easy access to MAP. In some areas, the number of abortions increased.

In a U.K. study of users of MAP, four out of the 12 women interviewed said their choice to have unprotected sexual intercourse was influenced by the knowledge that they could obtain the pill from a pharmacy.

In response to concern that providing the morning-after pill through pharmacists would lead to more unprotected sex, a user of the pill disclosed: "To be honest, in a way, that is what happened to me. I did previously know that X chemist was just over the road and I think, I think if I hadn't have known . . . if I hadn't have known I could have got it so easily, I would have been more careful, to be honest."

Risks to Adolescents

Many teenagers would be less confident in resisting sexual pressure, particularly if easy access to the pill is in the aggressor's arsenal of coercion. It will increase the likelihood of sexual abuse of girls, and that sexual perpetrators will prolong their rapes undetected.

Adolescents are unlikely to recognize if they have medical contraindications, less likely to follow directions for administration or to fully understand a medication label. They are less prone to seek medical

The author of this viewpoint argues that over-the-counter access to emergency contraceptives can lead to an increase in sexual exploitation.

help if they suffer symptoms of complications after secretly taking the MAP, and would not be aware that it lacks adequate testing.

Rather than reducing the core problem of young people engaging in sexual activity (which carries life-long consequences), it encourages sexual activity. An official survey revealed that MAP use among teenage girls in the United Kingdom more than doubled since it became available in pharmacies, increasing from one in 12 teen-agers to one in five. Among them were girls as young as 12. A girl who said she was 10 years old told the pharmacist "she had already used it four times."

Even morning-after pill proponents agree that sexually active girls are likely victims of sexual abuse, and interaction with medical professionals is an important defense.

> The Alan Guttmacher Institute reported: "The younger women are when they first have intercourse the more likely they are to have had unwanted or nonvoluntary first sex, seven in 10 of those who had sex before age 13, for example."
>
> "The possibility of sexual abuse should be considered routinely in every adolescent female patient who has initiated sexual activity,"

stated Dr. Joycelyn Elders in the *Journal of the American Medical Association.* The rush to choose "pregnancy outcome options" may preempt efforts to rule out sexual abuse. "Sexual abuse is a common antecedent of adolescent pregnancy, with up to 66% of pregnant teens reporting histories of abuse. . . . Pregnancy may also be a sign of ongoing sexual abuse. . . . Boyer and Fine found that of 535 young women who were pregnant, 44% had been raped, of whom 11% became pregnant as a result of the rape. One half of these young women with rape histories were raped more than once."

Tool for Abusers

The *Bangkok Post* reported disturbing consequences of easy availability of the morning-after pill for the past 15 years, including:

- Random studies showed that men are the most frequent buyers. "They buy the pills for their girlfriends or wives so that they don't have to wear condoms and feel they're at no risk of becoming a father afterwards. Some women I've spoken to said that they didn't even know what they were taking; that the guy just said it was a health supplement," said Nattaya Boonpakdee, program assistant at the Population Council (an agency dedicated to promoting and developing contraception and abortion methods).
- "Although many feminists believe that the morning-after pill gives them more control over their own bodies, it would seem, judging from the few studies conducted so far, that it is actually being used by men to exploit women."

EVALUATING THE AUTHOR'S ARGUMENTS:

In this viewpoint Wendy Wright finds ads for Plan B, a morning-after pill, objectionable because she thinks they promote wanton sexuality. Do you agree with her that the advertisements promote promiscuity, or do you think they depict the realities of the modern sexual world and offer Plan B as a way for women to protect themselves in it? Explain your perspective.

Facts About Birth Control

Editor's note: These facts can be used in reports or papers to reinforce or add credibility when making important points or claims.

History of Birth Control in the United States

- The Comstock Act of 1873 was used to prohibit the distribution of information about birth control.
- In 1914 Margaret Sanger published the *Woman Rebel*, which promoted use of contraception.
- In 1916 Margaret Sanger opened the first birth control clinic in America in Brooklyn, New York.
- Margaret Sanger founded the American Birth Control League in 1921, which later became the Planned Parenthood Federation of America.
- The modern condom was invented in the 1920s, but an early version of the condom appears in a cave painting in France that is fifteen thousand years old.
- In 1960 the Food and Drug Administration (FDA) approved use of the birth control pill, called Enovid.
- The contraceptive sponge was introduced in 1983.
- The first female condom went on the market in 1994.
- The Public Broadcasting Service provides the following facts about the history of birth control in the United States:
  - In 1954 fifty women in Massachusetts became the first human test subjects to take the pill, despite the state's strict anti–birth control laws.
  - 100 percent of the women who took the pill for the study did not ovulate.
  - In 1957 the FDA approved the use of Enovid, the first birth control pill, for menstrual disorders in women, but required the label carrying a warning that it prevented ovulation.
  - By 1959 more than five hundred thousand women were taking Enovid.

- In 1960 Enovid generated $37 million in revenue.
- The FDA approved Enovid for sale as a contraceptive in 1960.
- 1.2 million women were on the pill in 1962.
- 2.3 million women were on the pill in 1963.
- By 1964 one in four couples chose the pill as their form of contraception, making it the most popular form of birth control.
- In 1964 it was illegal to sell the pill in eight states.
- 6.5 million women were taking the pill in 1965.
- In 1965 Enovid sales generated $85 million.
- By 1968 women could choose from seven different birth control pill options.
- The pill became available to unmarried couples in 1972.

Teenagers and Birth Control in the United States
The Guttmacher Institute has found the following about teenagers who use birth control:
- Sexually active teens who do not use birth control have a 90 percent chance of getting pregnant within a year.
- 74 percent of females used contraception the first time they had sex.
- 82 percent of males used contraception the first time they had sex.
- 71 percent of males used a condom the first time they had sex.
- 66 percent of females used a condom the first time they had sex.
- Approximately 25 percent of sexually active teens use two methods of birth control during sex.
- 70 percent of teens would not get birth control from a clinic if they needed their parents' permission.

A 2008 study conducted by the Bradley Hasbro Children's Research Center found:
- Two-thirds of sexually active teenagers between ages fifteen and twenty-one did not use a condom the last time they had sex.
- More than 25 percent of participants did not use condoms during the previous three months of sexual activity.

In 2006 researchers from Columbia University and the Guttmacher Institute released a study that attributed 86 percent of the decline in teen pregnancy rates from 1995 to 2002 to contraception education. The National Youth Risk Behavior Survey found:

- The percentage of teens in grades nine through twelve who were sexually active dropped from 54.1 percent in 1991 to 46.8 percent in 2005.
- Teen condom use increased during that time from 46.2 percent to 62.8 percent.

Birth Control and Sexually Transmitted Diseases

A study released by the Centers for Disease Control in 2008 found that one in four girls between fourteen and nineteen years old has an STD.

A 2007 study conducted by the Washington, DC, school system concluded that many of the teenaged participants did not realize the pill does not protect them from STDs.

According to evidence presented at the 2004 STD Prevention Conference, STD rates are equal among teens who pledge virginity to those who do not make the pledge to remain abstinent until marriage.

Family Planning Perspectives found that 23 percent of teachers taught abstinence as the only way to prevent pregnancy and STDs in 2005.

According to a 2006 study published in the *New England Journal of Medicine*, females are 70 percent less likely to contract HPV when their male partners wear condoms each time during intercourse.

Efficacy of the Male Condom, the Pill, and Emergency Contraception

According to the Centers for Disease Control, the male condom is between 85 to 98 percent effective for preventing pregnancy.

According to Planned Parenthood:

- Less than 1 percent of women who take the pill every day get pregnant.

- The pill is 99.9 percent effective in preventing pregnancy.
- Of women who occasionally miss a dose, eight out of one hundred will get pregnant.
- Starting birth control pills within three days of having unprotected sex reduces a woman's chance of getting pregnant by 75 percent.
- Two out of one hundred women become pregnant when birth control pills are used as emergency contraception within three days of having unprotected sex.
- Taking an emergency contraceptive within seventy-two hours of having unprotected sex reduced a woman's chance of getting pregnant by 89 percent.
- If emergency contraception is taken within three days of having unprotected sex, only one out of one hundred women will become pregnant.

Abstinence Education in the United States

In 2006 researchers from Columbia University and the Guttmacher Institute concluded that 14 percent of the decline in teen pregnancy rates from 1995 to 2002 was due to abstinence-only education.

Since 1996 the Silver Ring Thing—a Christian-based abstinence education group—has persuaded fifty thousand kids and teenagers to wear purity rings.

According to a 2004 AP/Long Island/*Newsday* study:
- 99 percent of teenagers who did not pledge to remain abstinent had sex before getting married.
- 88 percent of teenagers who pledged abstinence had sex before marriage.

According to the National Campaign to Prevent Teen and Unplanned Pregnancy:
- 93 percent of parents believe abstinence education is important.
- 90 percent of teenagers believe abstinence education is important.
- 73 percent of adults think a combination of abstinence and contraception education is important.

- 56 percent of teens think a combination of abstinence and contraception education is important.

There are currently at least seven hundred abstinence-only education programs in the United States, as reported by the *New York Times*.

The *Los Angeles Times* reports that in the past eleven years, the federal government has spent more than $1.3 billion dollars on abstinence education.

According to the American Public Health Association:
- Thirty-three states receive federal funds for abstinence-only education programs.
- Seventeen states refuse federal funding for abstinence-only education programs.

A 2008 study by the Heritage Foundation found that eleven of fifteen abstinence education programs reviewed significantly delayed teens from having sex.

Organizations to Contact

The editors have compiled the following list of organizations concerned with the issues debated in this book. The descriptions are derived from materials provided by the organizations. All have publications or information available for interested readers. The list was compiled on the date of publication of the present volume; the information provided here may change. Be aware that many organizations take several weeks or longer to respond to queries, so allow as much time as possible.

ACLU Reproductive Freedom Project
125 Broad St., 18th Floor
New York, NY 10004-2400
(212) 549-2500
Web site: www.aclu.org/reproductiverights

This is a branch of the American Civil Liberties Union that works to guarantee the constitutional right to reproductive choice. The project produces fact sheets, pamphlets, articles, and reports, and publishes the quarterly newsletter *Reproductive Rights Update.*

Advocates for Youth
2000 M. St. NW, Ste. 250
Washington, DC 20036
(202) 419-3420
e-mail: info@advocatesforyouth.org
Web site: www.advocatesforyouth.org

Advocates for Youth is the only national organization focusing solely on pregnancy and HIV prevention among young people. It provides information, education, and advocacy to youth-serving agencies and professionals, policy makers, and the media. Among the organization's numerous publications are the brochures *Advice from Teens on Buying Condoms* and *Spread the Word—Not the Virus.* The organization has also launched numerous contraception campaigns to get the word out to teens about the importance of using condoms and the benefits of making emergency contraception available over the counter.

Alan Guttmacher Institute
125 Maiden Ln.
New York, NY 10038
(212) 248-1111
e-mail: info@agi-usa.org
Web site: www.agi-usa.org

The institute works to protect and expand the reproductive choices of all women and men. It strives to ensure that people have access to the information and services they need to exercise their rights and responsibilities concerning sexual activity, reproduction, and family planning. Among the institute's publications are the books *Emergency Contraception Has Tremendous Potential in the Fight to Reduce Unintended Pregnancy* and *Striking a Balance Between a Provider's Right to Refuse and a Patient's Right to Receive Care.*

Catholics for a Free Choice (CFFC)
1436 U St. NW, Ste. 301
Washington, DC 20009
(202) 986-6093
e-mail: cffc@catholicsforchoice.org
Web site: www.cath4choice.org

This organization promotes family planning to reduce the need for abortion and to increase women's choices in childbearing and child rearing. It publishes the bimonthly newsletter *Conscience.*

Child Trends, Inc. (CT)
4301 Connecticut Ave. NW, Ste. 350
Washington, DC 20008
(202) 572-6000
Web site: www.childtrends.org

CT works to analyze contraceptive use among teens and uses statistics and research to educate the teenage population to become consistent users of contraception. The organization produces many publications, including *Facts at a Glance*, which incorporates city, state, and national statistics on teen pregnancy, childbearing, and sexuality.

Coalition for Positive Sexuality (CPS)
PO Box 77212
Washington, DC 20013
(773) 604-1654
Web site: www.positive.org

The Coalition for Positive Sexuality is a grassroots, direct-action group formed in the spring of 1992 by high school students and activists. CPS works to counteract the institutionalized misogyny, heterosexism, homophobia, racism, and ageism that students experience every day at school. It is dedicated to offering teens sexuality and safe sex education that is pro-woman, pro-lesbian/gay/bisexual, pro-safe sex, and pro-choice. Its motto is, "Have fun and be safe." CPS publishes the pamphlet *Just Say Yes.*

Family Research Council (FRC)
801 G St. NW
Washington, DC 20001
(202) 393-2100
e-mail: corrdept@frc.org
Web site: www.frc.org

The council is a research, resource, and education organization that promotes the traditional family. It opposes condom distribution programs in schools, and among the council's numerous publications are the papers "Revolt of the Virgins," "Abstinence: The New Sexual Revolution," and "Abstinence Programs Show Promise in Reducing Sexual Activity and Pregnancy Among Teens."

Focus on the Family
Colorado Springs, CO 80995
(719) 531-5181
Web site: www.fotf.org

Focus on the Family is an organization that promotes Christian values and strong family ties. It campaigns for abstinence until marriage and is opposed to any form of birth control that interferes with fertilization, such as the IUD. It has no official position on birth control pills, but it is opposed to emergency contraception. It publishes the monthly magazine *Focus on the Family* and sells many books on its Web site that promote abstinence, such as *Wait for Me: Rediscovering the Purity of Joy in Romance.*

Healthy Teen Network
1501 St. Paul St., Ste. 124
Baltimore, MD 21202
(410) 685-0481
Web site: www.healthyteennetwork.org

Healthy Teen Network is a national organization that focuses on adolescent health issues and is committed to preventing teen pregnancy. It is a network of health specialists, therapists, and reproductive health-care professionals that supports sexual health for teens at the city, state, and federal level. It puts out many publications, including *Helping Teens Stay Healthy and Safe: Birth Control and Confidential Services* and *A Tool to Assess the Characteristics of Effective Sex and STD/HIV Education Programs.*

The Heritage Foundation
214 Massachusetts Ave. NE
Washington, DC 20002
(202) 546-4400
e-mail: info@heritage.org
Web site: www.heritage.org

The Heritage Foundation is a public policy research institute that supports the ideas of limited government and the free-market system. It promotes the view that the welfare system has contributed to the problems of illegitimacy and teenage pregnancy. Some of the foundation's numerous publications include "Abstinence Education: Assessing the Evidence," "Adolescent Virginity Pledges, Condom Use, and Sexually Transmitted Diseases Among Young Adults," and "Adolescent Virginity Pledges and Risky Sexual Behaviors."

National Abortion and Reproductive Rights Action League (NARAL)
1156 Fifteenth St. NW, Ste. 700

Washington, DC 20005
(202) 973-3000
e-mail: comments@naral.org
Web site: www.prochoiceamerica.org

NARAL is the nation's leading advocate for privacy and a woman's right to affordable birth control. NARAL works to protect the pro-choice values of freedom and privacy while reducing the need for abortions. It publishes numerous articles, pamphlets, reports, and news briefs about the state of women's access to birth control in America.

National Campaign to Prevent Teen Pregnancy
1176 Massachusetts Ave. NW
Washington, DC 20036
(202) 478-8500
Web site: www.teenpregnancy.org

The mission of the National Campaign is to reduce teenage and unplanned pregnancy by promoting a combination of abstinence and contraception education for adolescents. The campaign publishes pamphlets, brochures, and opinion polls that include *Not Yet: Programs to Delay First Sex Among Teens, The Next Best Thing: Helping Sexually Active Teens Avoid Pregnancy,* and *What Helps in Providing Contraceptive Services to Teens?*

Planned Parenthood Federation of America (PPFA)
434 West 33rd St.
New York, NY 10011
(212) 541-7800
e-mail: communications@ppfa.org
Web site: www.plannedparenthood.org

Planned Parenthood believes individuals have the right to control their own fertility without governmental interference. It promotes comprehensive sex education and provides contraceptive counseling and services through clinics across the United States. Its publications include the brochures *Guide to Birth Control: Seven Accepted Methods of Contraception, Teen Sex? It's Okay to Say No Way,* and the bimonthly newsletter *LinkLine.*

Project Reality
170 E. Lake Ave., Ste. 371
Glenview, IL 60025
(847) 729-3298
e-mail: preality@pair.com
Web site: www.projectreality.org

Project Reality promotes an abstinence education curriculum for junior and senior high students. The program is designed to present the benefits of abstinence by using a combination of educational materials and presentations. Research, facts, and statistics are incorporated into the curriculum to demonstrate the dangers of having sex before marriage. The organization works to make teenagers feel pride in their choice to remain abstinent and equips them with the skills to say no to sex.

Religious Coalition for Reproductive Choice
1025 Vermont Ave. NW, Ste. 1130
Washington, DC 20005
(202) 628-7700
e-mail: info@rcrc.org
Web site: www.rcrc.org

The coalition works to inform the media and the public that many mainstream religions support reproductive options, including birth control. It works to make birth control affordable to America's poorest citizens and supports the Prevention Through Affordable Access Act as well as the Responsible Education About Life Act. The coalition also publishes "The Role of Religious Congregations in Fostering Adolescent Sexual Health."

**Sexuality Information and Education Council
of the United States (SIECUS)**
90 John St., Ste. 704

New York, NY 10038
(212) 819-9770
e-mail: pmalone@siecus.org
Web site: www.siecus.org

SIECUS is an organization of educators, physicians, social workers, and others who support the individual's right to acquire knowledge of sexuality and who encourage responsible sexual behavior. The council promotes comprehensive sex education for all children that includes AIDS education, teaching about homosexuality, and instruction about contraceptives and sexually transmitted diseases. Its publications include fact sheets, annotated bibliographies by topic, the booklet *Talk About Sex*, and the monthly *SIECUS Report*.

Teen-Aid
723 E. Jackson Ave.
Spokane, WA 99207
(509) 482-2868
e-mail: teenaid@teen-aid.org
Web site: www.teen-aid.org

Teen-Aid is an international organization that promotes traditional family values and sexual morality. It promotes abstinence as "saying 'yes' to the rest of your life," and publishes a public school sex education curriculum, *Sexuality, Commitment and Family*, stressing abstinence before marriage. It also publishes several articles, including "Abstinence Education: Setting the Record Straight," and "An Abstinence Program's Impact on Cognitive Mediators and Sexual Initiation."

Teen STAR Program
Natural Family Planning Center of Washington, DC
8514 Bradmoor Dr.
Bethesda, MD 20817
(301) 897-9323
e-mail: hannaklaus@earthlink.net
Web site: www.teenstar-international.org

Teen STAR (Sexuality Teaching in the context of Adult Responsibility) is an international program geared for early, middle, and late adolescence. Classes are designed to foster understanding of the body and its fertility pattern and to explore the emotional, cognitive, social, and spiritual aspects of human sexuality. Teen STAR believes that preaching abstinence and promoting condoms are ineffective ways to educate teens to act sexually responsible. It publishes a bimonthly newsletter and the paper "Sexual Behavior of Youth: How to Influence It."

For Further Reading

Books

Robert Engelman, *More: Population, Nature, and What Women Want.* Washington DC: Island, 2008. Examines how a woman's right to choose whether to have children—and how many—affects the world at large.

Linda Gordon, *The Moral Property of Women: A History of Birth Control Politics in America.* Champaign: University of Illinois Press, 2007. Offers a comprehensive history of the pro– and anti–birth control movement.

John W. Johnson, *Griswold V. Connecticut: Birth Control and the Constitutional Right of Privacy.* Lawrence: University Press of Kansas, 2005. Discusses how this landmark Supreme Court decision protects birth control under the right to privacy.

Robert Jüette, *Contraception: A History.* Cambridge, UK: Polity, 2008. Examines the personal, social, and political history of birth control from before the Middle Ages through the twentieth century.

Stephen Mosher, *Population Control: Real Costs, Illusory Benefits.* Piscataway, NJ: Transaction, 2008. Argues that efforts to control population are causing a dangerous global decline in fertility.

Johanna Schoen, *Choice and Coercion: Birth Control, Sterilization, and Abortion in Public Health and Welfare.* Chapel Hill: University of North Carolina Press, 2005. Explores how state and national polices affect women's control over reproduction.

Halliday G. Sutherland, *Birth Control: A Statement of Christian Doctrine Against the Neo-Malthusians.* Whitefish, MT: Kessinger, 2004. Argues that using birth control is in direct opposition to the Divine Will to procreate.

Periodicals

Carla Adams, "SPEAKOUT: Abstinence Education Has Been Effective," *Rocky Mountain News,* March 19, 2008. www.rockymountainnews .com/news/2008/mar/19/speakout-abstinence-education-has-been-effective.

Eric Alterman and George Zornick, "Think Again: The Costs of Enforced Sexual Ignorance," Center for American Progress, May 8, 2008. www .americanprogress.org/issues/2008/05/alterman_ignorance.html.

BBC.com, "The Ethical Problems of Mass Birth Control Programmes." www.bcc.co.uk/ethics/contraception/mass_birth_control_1 .shtml?did=2332.

Laura Billings, "Speaking of Sex," Mspmag.com, October 2007. www .mspmag.com/health/fitforlife/78349_2.asp.

Sarah Carey, "Give Me the Pill, Not a Lecture," *Sunday Times*, October 29, 2006.

Kathy Clay-Little, "In the Real World, the Facts About Sex Are Necessary," *San Antonio Express-News*, October 8, 2007.

Norman A. Constantine, "Converging Evidence Leaves Policy Behind: Sex Education in the United States," *Journal of Adolescent Health*, April 2008.

DailyWildcat.com, "Parental Consent Bill Dangerous," February 23, 2006. http://media.wildcat.arizona.edu/media/storage/ paper997/news/2006/02/23/Opinions/Parental.Consent.Bill .Dangerous-1625118.shtml.

Sara Sturmon Dale, "Can a Pharmacist Refuse to Dispense Birth Control?" *Time*, May 30, 2004. www.time.com/time/magazine/ article/0,9171,1101040607-644153,00.html.

Moira Gaul, "Testimony on D.C. Public Schools Sex Education," Family Research Council, November 30, 2007. www.frc.org/get .cfm?i=TS07L01.

Francie Grace, "Study Says Sexually Active Teens Using Birth Control Less Often," Publicagenda.org, June 5, 2008. www.publicagenda.org/ blogs/study-says-sexually-active-teens-using-birth-control-less-often.

Marybeth Hicks, "This Mom's Not Ready for Birth Control in Schools," *Washington Times*, November 4, 2007.

Priya Jain, "The Battle to Ban Birth Control," Salon.com, March 20, 2006. www.salon.com/mwt/feature/2006/03/20/anti_contraception.

Sue Katz, "Maybe We Should Outsource Our Sex Education to Mexico," Alternet.org, June 4, 2008. www.alternet.org/sex/87052.

Susan Kelley-Stamerra, "Children Deserve a Sex Education Policy That Provides Answers," *Huffington Post*, September 22, 2008. www

.huffingtonpost.com/susan-kelleystamerra/children-deserve-a-sex-ed_b_128415.html.

Deborah Kotz, "A Government Threat to Birth Control," *U.S. News & World Report*, June 22, 2008. http://health.usnews.com/articles/health/womens-health/2008/07/22/a-government-threat-to-birth-control.html.

Dahlia Lithwick, "Martyrs and Pestles," Slate.com, April 13, 2005. www.slate.com/id/2116688.

R. Albert Mohler Jr., "Can Christians Use Birth Control?" *Christian Post*, May 8, 2006. www.christianpost.com/article/20060508/can-christians-use-birth-control.htm.

MSNBC.com, "Maine Middle School to Offer Birth Control," October 18, 2007. www.msnbc.msn.com/id/21358971.

NARAL Pro-Choice America, "Emergency Contraception Can Help Reduce the Teen-Pregnancy Rate," December 1, 2007. www.prochoiceamerica.org/assets/files/Birth-Control-EC-teens.pdf.

———, "Insurance Coverage for Contraception: A Proven Way to Protect and Promote Women's Health," December 1, 2007. www.prochoiceamerica.org/assets/files/Birth-Control-Insurance-Coverage.pdf.

Planned Parenthood, "Equity in Prescription Insurance and Contraceptive Coverage," April 17, 2007. www.plannedparenthood.org/issues-action/birth-control/insurance-coverage-for-birth-control/reports/prescription-insurance-6548.htm.

Population Research Institute, "Emergency Contraception and the Dangers to Adolescents," March 5, 2004. www.pop.org/main.cfm?id=215&r1=2.00&r2=1.50&r3=0.05&r4=0&level=3&eid=547.

Robert E. Rector, Melissa G. Pardue, and Shannan Martin, "What Do Parents Want Taught in Sex Education Programs?" Heritage Foundation, January 28, 2004. www.heritage.org/research/abstinence/bg1722.cfm.

ScienceDaily, "Comprehensive Sex Education Might Reduce Teen Pregnancies, Study Suggests," March 20, 2008. www.sciencedaily.com/releases/2008/03/080319151225.htm.

Russell Shorto, "Contra-Contraception," *New York Times Magazine,* May 7, 2006. www.nytimes.com/2006/05/07/magazine/07contraception .html.

Laura Sessions Stepp, "For Some Teens, a Checkup Just Isn't Macho," *Washington Post,* April 17, 2007. www.washingtonpost.com/wp-dyn/ content/article/2007/04/14/AR2007041400222.html.

Susan Yudt, "Why Teens Need Emergency Contraception," Teenwire.com, May 21, 2004. www.teenwire.com/infocus/2004/ if-20040521p291-EC.php.

Web Sites

Abstinence Clearinghouse (www.abstinence.net). The Abstinence Clearinghouse is a nonprofit Web site that seeks to provide resources at a central location to those interested in abstinence programs and education. The Web site provides hundreds of resources for those seeking to remain abstinent until marriage. It also contains a blog where authors discuss the impact of society on teens and sexuality.

Contraceptive Information Resource (www.contracept.org). CIR exists to provide the most up-to-date information on contraception for both men and women. The Web site is designed to educate its readers about the efficacy and failures of various birth control methods as well as assist people with their family planning goals. CIR also provides facts, statistics, and research to help its readers make informed decisions about their sexual health.

It's Great to Wait (www.greattowait.com). This Web site set up by the Florida Department of Health encourages teenagers to practice abstinence by teaching kids how to say "no" to sex. The site teaches teens that having self-respect makes it easy to avoid giving in to peer pressure to have sex. Personal stories of teens are included, ranging from those who have committed to wait until marriage to have sex to those who accidentally got pregnant. There are resources for teens, parents, and educators as well as a calendar of abstinence-only events.

The Mayo Clinic (www.mayoclinic.com/health/birth-control/ BI99999). The award-winning Web site of the Mayo Foundation provides information on a variety of health topics, including sexual health, abstinence, and methods of contraception. The Web site relies on the talents and expertise of more than thirty-four hundred doctors and scientists to compile its information.

MedlinePlus (www.nlm.nih.gov/medlineplus/birthcontrol.html). MedlinePlus is a Web service of the U.S. National Library of Medicine and the National Institutes of Health. Its section on birth control offers information and links to types of birth control, research and statistics on efficacy, and the latest news in reproductive health.

The National Women's Health Information Center (http://women shealth.gov). This Web site was established by the U.S. Department of Health and Human Services Office of Women's Health to give free access to gender-specific health information to women and girls. Information is available on a wide range of topics, including birth control and emergency contraception.

Teens Health (http://kidshealth.org/teen/sexual_health/contraception/contraception.html). This Nemours Foundation Web site discusses the choices teens face when confronted with the decision to have sex. Topics covered include general information about birth control as well as on specific methods of contraception, such as the pill, the patch, the ring, injections, and condoms.

Index

Picture Credits

IVAN ALVARADO/Reuters/Landov, 59

© Angela Hampton Picture Library/Alamy, 10

AP Images, 53, 78

© Paul Baldesare/Alamy, 50

Bradley C. Bower/Bloomberg News/Landov, 66

Image copyright Deklofenak, 2009. Used under license from Shutterstock.com, 74

© Michael A. Keller/zefa/Corbis, 85

© Bobbie Lerryn/Alamy, 47

© Dennis MacDonald/Alamy, 25

Spencer Platt/Getty Images, 14

© SuperStock, Inc./SuperStock, 70

UPI Photo/Landov, 89

Abel Uribe/MCT/Landov, 33

Ian Waldie/Getty Images, 21

© Tony West/Alamy, 99

© David White/Alamy, 37

Steve Zmina, 19, 26, 31, 40, 45, 54, 63, 72, 83, 91